MW01030050

# Kindergarten
## Essentials

Thinking Kids®
Carson-Dellosa Publishing LLC
Greensboro, North Carolina

Thinking Kids®
An imprint of Carson-Dellosa Publishing LLC
P.O. Box 35665
Greensboro, NC 27425  USA

Printed in the USA • All rights reserved.                    ISBN  978-1-4838-3817-5

04-147191151

# Table of Contents

# Welcome to the *Essentials* series!

Building a strong foundation is an essential part of your child's everyday success. This series features a variety of activity pages that make learning fun, keeping your child engaged and entertained at the same time. These colorful workbooks will help children meet important proficiency standards with activities that strengthen their basic skills, math, and reading.

With the *Essentials* series, learning isn't just contained to the pages of the workbook. Each activity offers "One Step Further," a suggestion for children to continue the learning activity on their own. This encourages children to take what they've learned and apply it to everyday situations, reinforcing their comprehension of the activity while exploring the world around them, preparing them with the skills needed to succeed in the 21st century.

These books provide an outstanding educational experience and important learning tools to prepare your child for the future. The *Essentials* series offers hours of educational entertainment that will make your child want to come back for more!

INTRODUCTION

# Basic Skills

SIZES

COLORS

OPPOSITES

RIGHT

SHAPES

# Same

**Directions:** Color the shape in each row that looks the same as the first shape.

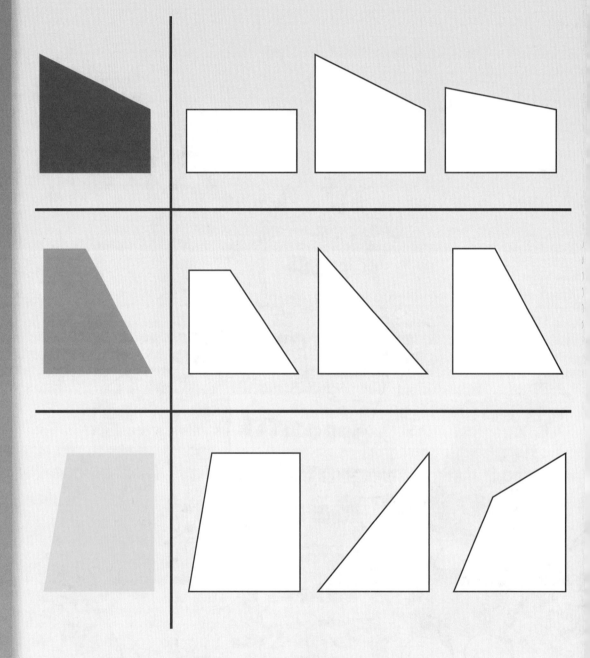

## One Step Further

Find two objects in your home that are the same shape. What shape are those objects?

# Different

**Directions:** Draw an **X** on the shapes in each row that are different from the first shape.

## One Step Further
Find a green object and a blue object.
Are they the same shape?

# Holiday Match

**Directions:** Color the first picture. Color each picture that is the **same** as the first one.

## One Step Further

Make a holiday card for a friend. Use some of the pictures you see on this page.

BASIC SKILLS

# A Complete Picture

**Directions:** Draw the missing parts to make the pictures look the same. Color the pictures with the same colors.

BASIC SKILLS

## One Step Further

Draw a picture. Ask a friend to draw a picture that looks the same as yours.

# Dinosaur Match

**Directions:** Draw a line to match each dinosaur with its skeleton.

## One Step Further

Where can you see dinosaurs today?
Which dinosaur on this page is your favorite?

# Shadow Shapes

**Directions:** Look at the shadow shapes in the first row. Draw a line from each shadow to the picture it matches.

## One Step Further

Draw what your shadow might look like if you are standing on one leg.

Kindergarten Essentials

# Same and Different

**Directions:** Color the two pictures in each row that are the same.

## One Step Further

Find two shirts that you own.
Describe what is different about them.

**BASIC SKILLS**

# Basketball!

Coby loves to play basketball. In fact, he has six pairs of sneakers just for basketball!

**Directions:** Draw a line to connect each pair of matching shoes.

## One Step Further

Find a pair of shoes in your home that match. Then, find two shoes that don't match.

Kindergarten Essentials

# Pete the Peacock

Look at Pete the Peacock.

**Directions:** Only one of the peacocks below is exactly like Pete. Circle it. What is different about each of the other peacocks?

## One Step Further
Draw another peacock.
Color each of its feathers a different color.

# Butterfly, Butterflies

A butterfly is a type of insect. It has four wings. Only two of the butterflies below look the same.

**Directions:** Can you find the two matching butterflies? Draw a line to connect them.

## One Step Further
Can you find two things in your neighborhood that look the same?

Kindergarten Essentials

# Opposites

**Opposites** are things that are different in every way.

**Directions:** Draw a line to match the opposites.

day

little

front

sad

happy

night

big

back

## One Step Further

Look around your home. Find something that is big. Then, find something that is little.

Kindergarten Essentials

# Opposites

**Directions:** Draw a line to match the opposites.

old

girl

boy

full

open

new

empty

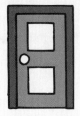

closed

### One Step Further

Look around your neighborhood for something that is closed.

Kindergarten Essentials

# Fast and Slow

**Directions:** Look at the picture below. Circle the things that go fast. Draw an **X** on each thing that goes slow.

## One Step Further

Sit outside. What can you see that goes fast?
What can you see that goes slow?

# Full and Empty

**Directions:** Circle the full container. Draw an **X** on the empty container.

**One Step Further**
Fill a cup with water until it's full.
Then, dump the water out. Is the cup empty?

Kindergarten Essentials

# Taller and Shorter

**Directions:** Circle the picture that is taller. Draw an **X** on the picture that is shorter.

**One Step Further**
Stand next to a friend.
Are you taller or shorter?

# Above and Below

**Directions:** Circle the picture that is above the others. Draw an **X** on the picture that is below the others.

## One Step Further

Look up. What is above you?
Look down. What is below you?

# Thanksgiving Day!

Doug just helped his mom set all of the food on the table for Thanksgiving Day. Which things on the table are hot? Which things on the table are cold?

**Directions:** Circle all of the hot things with a **red** crayon. Circle all of the cold things with a **blue** crayon.

## One Step Further
Tell a friend about your favorite Thanksgiving celebration.

# Baseball

Belinda just went to her first baseball game. Many people sat in the bleachers watching it.

**Directions:** Which person is sitting on something soft? Color that person **pink**.
Which person is sitting on something hard? Color that person **purple**.
Which person is happy? Color that person **yellow**.
Which person is sad? Color that person **blue**.
Which person is short? Color that person **red**.
Which person is tall? Color that person **orange**.

**One Step Further**
Make up a story about what is happening in the picture. Do you like watching sports?

BASIC SKILLS

# Things That Go Together

**Directions:** Color the pictures in each row that go together. Draw an **X** on the one that does **not** belong.

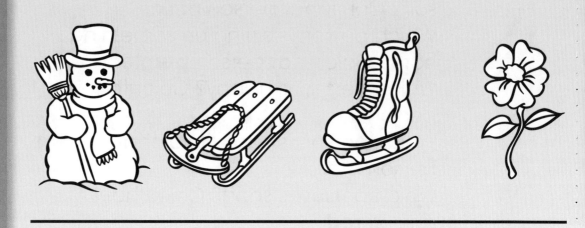

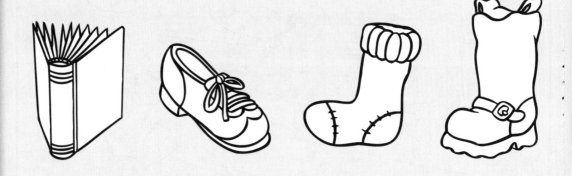

## One Step Further
Name something fun you can do in the snow.

# Part of a Group

**Directions:** Pick three pictures that go together in each group. Draw an **X** on the picture that does **not** belong in the group.

## One Step Further
Choose a picture that has an **X** on it. What is something that goes with that object?

Kindergarten Essentials

# You Choose

**Directions:** Look at the animals below.

Which animals have feathers?

Which animals have no legs?

Which animals would be fun to ride?

## One Step Further

Which of the animals on this page would make a good pet? What would you name it?

# The Jungle

Many animals live in the jungle.

**Directions:** Find the animals that are small.

Which animals are large?

Which animals do you think are scaly?

Which animals are soft?

**One Step Further**
Name another jungle animal.
Describe that animal to a friend.

# So Soft

**Directions:** Which objects below are soft? Color all of the soft things **red**. Color the rest of the objects in a way that makes sense.

## One Step Further

Look around your bedroom for something soft. What did you find?

# Creepy Caves

Many different kinds of animals live in dark caves. Some of the animals pictured below live in caves and some do not. Which animals do not belong?

**Directions:** Draw an **X** on the animals that do **not** belong in a cave.

BASIC SKILLS

**One Step Further**

Where do the other animals on this page live?

Kindergarten Essentials

# What Goes Together?

**Directions:** Draw a line to match each thing that goes together.

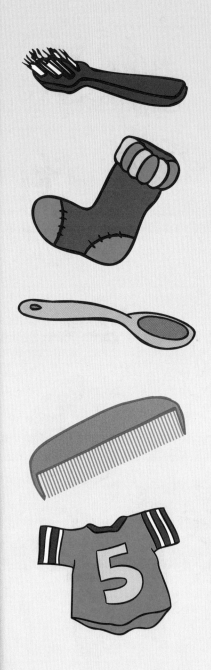

## One Step Further

Look around your bedroom.
Find two more objects that go together.

# Three Things

**Directions:** Circle your answers below.

Which three things are on your hand?

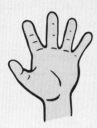   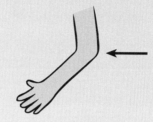

Which three things are in the sky?

   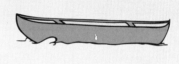

Which three things would you wear if you were hot?

## One Step Further
What is your favorite thing to do when it's hot outside?

BASIC SKILLS

# Letter Recognition

**Directions:** Circle the letters in each row that match the first letter.

| A | N | A | V | A |
|---|---|---|---|---|
| a | b | a | c | a |
| B | B | C | B | A |
| b | d | a | b | a |
| C | O | C | D | C |
| c | a | c | c | o |

## One Step Further

Name an animal that starts with **A**, **B**, or **C**.
What color is that animal?

BASIC SKILLS

# Letter Recognition

**Directions:** Circle the letters in each row that match the first letter.

| | | | | | |
|---|---|---|---|---|---|
| **D** | B | G | D | D | B |
| **d** | b | d | a | d | |
| **E** | H | F | E | E | |
| **e** | e | a | b | e | |
| **F** | E | F | E | A | |
| **f** | t | f | l | o | |

**One Step Further**

Name a food that starts with **D**, **E**, or **F**.
When was the last time you ate that food?

# Letter Recognition

**Directions:** Circle the letters in each row that match the first letter.

| G | C | G | O | B |
|---|---|---|---|---|
| g | g | p | q | g |
| H | E | F | H | I |
| h | d | n | b | h |
| I | H | I | L | A |
| i | t | i | l | i |

## One Step Further

Name an object that is green or gray.
What letter does that object start with?

BASIC SKILLS

# Letter Recognition

**Directions:** Circle the letters in each row that match the first letter.

| J | J | U | L | J |
|---|---|---|---|---|
| j | g | j | q | i |
| K | N | F | H | K |
| k | l | h | k | b |
| L | J | I | L | U |
| I | t | i | l | i |

## One Step Further
Ask a friend to name something that starts with **J**, **K**, or **L**. Then, name a different object.

BASIC SKILLS

# Letter Recognition

**Directions:** Circle the letters in each row that match the first letter.

| M | H | M | n | L |
|---|---|---|---|---|
| m | M | a | m | n |
| N | M | N | m | N |
| n | n | m | a | n |
| O | O | D | B | O |
| o | a | O | C | o |

## One Step Further

Draw an oval. Draw something that starts with the letter **O** inside the oval.

BASIC SKILLS

# Letter Recognition

**Directions:** Circle the letters in each row that match the first letter.

| | | | | |
|---|---|---|---|---|
| P | D | P | O | b |
| p | p | d | q | b |
| Q | O | Q | G | Q |
| q | p | q | d | b |
| R | R | B | P | R |
| r | r | n | m | r |

**One Step Further**
Look around your bedroom for something that starts with **P**, **Q**, or **R**.

BASIC SKILLS

# Letter Recognition

**Directions:** Circle the letters in each row that match the first letter.

| | | | | | |
|---|---|---|---|---|---|
| **S** | P | S | B | S |
| **s** | o | a | s | e |
| **T** | I | P | L | T |
| **t** | f | l | t | i |
| **U** | U | D | U | O |
| **u** | n | m | n | |

## One Step Further

Name a friend or family member whose name starts with **S**, **T**, or **U**.

# Letter Recognition

**Directions:** Circle the letters in each row that match the first letter.

| V | W | V | A | N |
|---|---|---|---|---|
| V | w | X | v | y |
| W | V | M | A | W |
| w | w | v | x | m |
| X | Y | X | V | K |
| x | y | k | x | z |

**One Step Further**

Name an object that starts with **V**, **W**, or **X**. Describe that object and what you use it for.

Kindergarten Essentials

# Letter Recognition

**Directions:** Circle the letters in each row that match the first letter.

| Y | W | Y | V | X |
|---|---|---|---|---|
| y | W | X | V | y |
| Z | N | M | Z | W |
| z | n | z | x | m |

**One Step Further**
Draw a picture of a zebra you might
see during a day at the zoo.

# Rhyming Pairs

Words that have the same ending sounds are called **rhyming** words.

**Directions:** Circle the pairs that rhyme.

map          nest          dog          frog

hat          bat          kite          mop

can          fan          rat          pig

**One Step Further**
Name a word that rhymes with **map**.
Name two other rhyming words.

BASIC SKILLS

# Rhyming Pairs

**Directions:** Circle the pairs that rhyme.

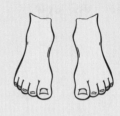

**nose**     **hose**          **beet**          **feet**

**star**      **jar**           **box**           **fox**

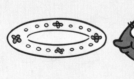

**dish**     **fish**          **cake**          **cap**

## One Step Further

Choose a word on this page.
Can you name an object that rhymes with it?

# Reading

# ABC Order

**Directions:** Connect the dots in ABC order. Color the picture.

READING

## One Step Further

Give the dog a name. Find an object that starts with the same letter as the dog's name.

# Buddy's Basket

Buddy is putting things in his basket. He wants only things that begin with **Bb**.

**Directions:** Color the pictures of things that begin with **Bb**.

**One Step Further**
Look around your room for objects to add to Buddy's basket.

# Todd's Toy Box

Todd's toy box only has toys that begin with **Tt**. Look at the toys below. Which ones belong in the box?

**Directions:** Draw lines from those toys to the box.

**One Step Further**
What other objects that begin with the **Tt** sound could go in Todd's toy box?

# A Super Slide

Help Sissy get down the slide.

**Directions:** Write the letter **s** in each space. Then, say each word aloud.

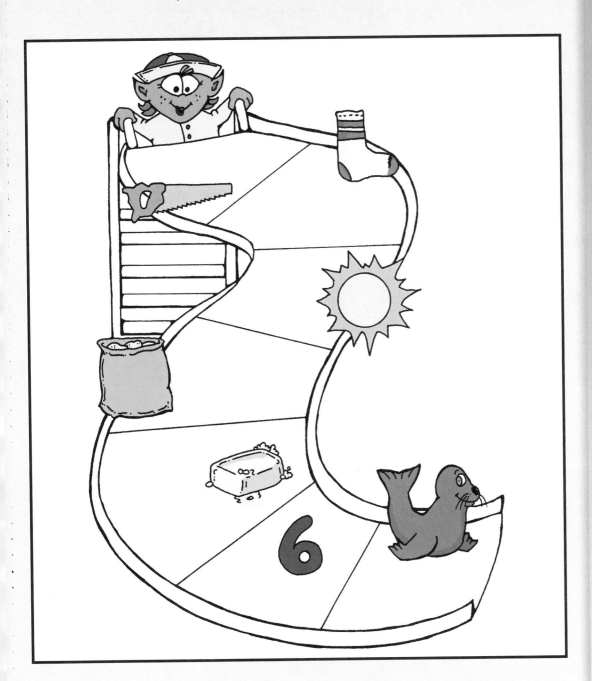

READING

## One Step Further
Slide on your feet across a tile floor.
Be careful not to slip!

# Crazy Caterpillar

Give the caterpillar some spots.

**Directions:** Say the name of each picture. If the picture name begins with the same sound as **caterpillar**, circle the picture to make a spot.

## One Step Further

What other words can you think of that start with the same sound as **caterpillar**?

# Mouse Magic

Help Michael Mouse perform magic.

**Directions:** Color only the pictures that begin with the sound of **Mm**.

### One Step Further
What other words can you think of that start with the **Mm** sound?

# Dixie's Drawings

Dixie drew pictures of things that begin with **Dd**. Look at the pictures below.

**Directions:** Circle the ones that Dixie drew.

## One Step Further

Draw a picture of you and a friend.
Are there any **Dd** words in the picture?

# Consonant Review

**Directions:** Write the beginning sound for each picture.

_____  _____  _____  _____

_____  _____  _____  _____

_____  _____  _____  _____

## One Step Further

Ask a friend to name an object.
What sound does that object begin with?

Kindergarten Essentials

READING

# Wonderful Wagon

The wagon can carry only pictures whose names begin with the sound of **Ww**.

**Directions:** Color the pictures that can go in the wagon.

## One Step Further

Look at a wall in the room you are in.
What is on the wall?

# Jump, Jake, Jump!

Help Jake jump along the path.

**Directions:** Write the letter **j** on the lines to complete the words. Then, say each word aloud.

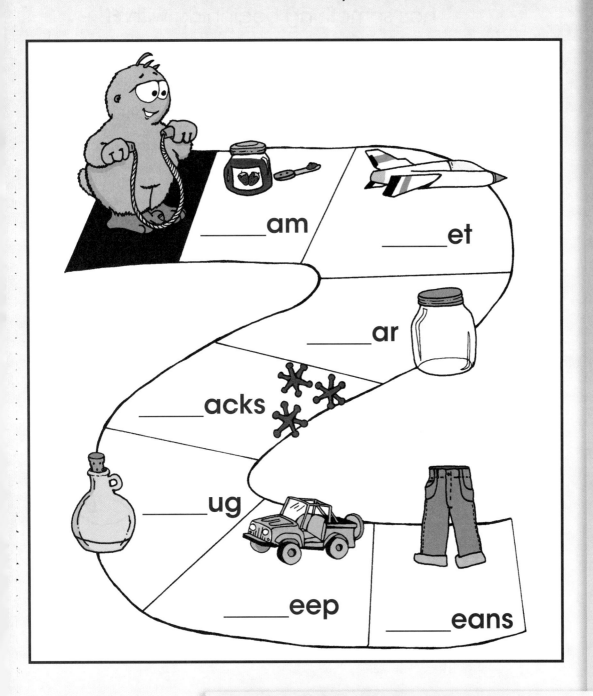

_____am

_____et

_____ar

_____acks

_____ug

_____eep

_____eans

**One Step Further**
Name a friend whose name starts with the letter **J**.

# Fishing Fun

These monsters are fishing for things that begin with **Ff**.

**Directions:** Draw a line from each hook to a fish that has something beginning with **Ff**.

**READING**

## One Step Further

What is your favorite food?
Draw food for the fish to eat.

Kindergarten Essentials

# Rain, Rain, Go Away

**Directions:** Color the raindrops that have pictures that begin with **Rr**.

## One Step Further

What is your favorite thing to do when it's raining?

# Pizza Party

Look at the picture.

**Directions:** Circle eight things that begin with **Pp**.

**One Step Further**
Tell a story about what is happening in the picture.

Kindergarten Essentials

# In Huey's House

Find the seven **Hh** things in Huey's house.

**Directions:** Color them **red**. Then, color the rest of the picture.

**One Step Further**
Find seven red things in your home.
Do any of them begin with the **Hh** sound?

# Handy Norman

Norman loves the letter **Nn**!

**Directions:** Draw a line from each of Norman's hands to a picture of something that begins with **Nn**.

## One Step Further
Grab a net and go outside.
What can you catch in the net?

# Special Keys

Each monster has a key. The keys will open only chests that have pictures of things beginning with **Kk**.

**Directions:** Circle the chests the keys will open.

READING

**One Step Further**
Ask an adult to give you a key.
Try to find out what it unlocks.

Kindergarten Essentials

# Very Vivid Vs

**Directions:** Draw a line from **Vv** to each picture that begins with the sound of **Vv**. Then, color the **Vv** pictures.

Vv

## One Step Further
Make a valentine for a friend. Decorate it using your favorite shapes and colors.

# Light It Up!

**Directions:** Draw a line from the light to each picture that begins with the sound of **Ll**. Then, color the **Ll** pictures.

**One Step Further**
Find an object in your home that starts with the **Ll** sound.

# A Great Garden of Gs

**Directions:** Write **g** under each picture that begins with the sound of **g**. Color thc **g** pictures.

   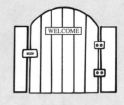

_____  _____  _____  _____

- - - - - - - - - - - - - - - - - - - - - - - -

_____  _____  _____  _____

_____  _____  _____  _____

- - - - - - - - - - - - - - - - - - - - - - - -

_____  _____  _____  _____

_____  _____  _____  _____

- - - - - - - - - - - - - - - - - - - - - - - -

_____  _____  _____  _____

## One Step Further
Look outside. What do you see that starts with the **Gg** sound?

# A Colorful Quilt

**Directions:** If the picture inside the quilt square begins with **Qq**, color it orange. If it does not, color it **purple**.

**READING**

## One Step Further

It's quiet time! Ask an adult to read to you. Are there any **Qq** words in the book?

*Kindergarten Essentials*

# Yolanda's Picture Chart

Help Yolanda finish her picture chart.

**Directions:** Write **y** on the lines to complete the words. Then, say each word aloud.

_____o-yo

_____olk

_____ak

_____ard

_____arn

_____ellow

## One Step Further

Draw a picture of the sun. Color it yellow.
Is the sun shining right now?

# Zep Zebra's Zoo

Zep Zebra likes living in the zoo.

**Directions:** Color each picture that begins with the sound of **Zz**.

## One Step Further

Tell a story about a day at the zoo.
What is your favorite zoo animal?

# Consonant Review

Say the name of each picture.

**Directions:** Write the letter that makes the beginning sound.

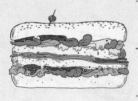

## One Step Further

What letter does your name start with?
Is that letter a consonant?

# Amazing As

**Directions:** Draw a line from each apple to a picture that begins with the sound of **Aa**. Draw an **X** on the picture that does **not** belong. Color the **Aa** pictures.

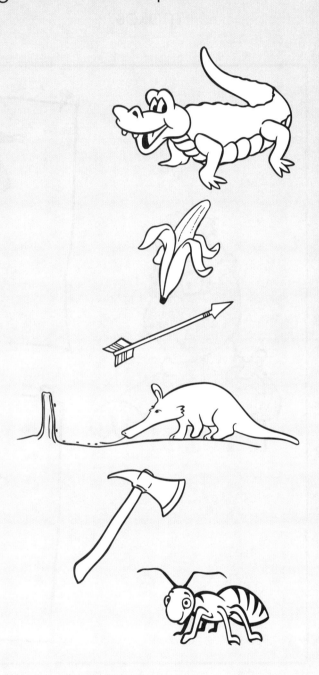

### One Step Further
Eat an apple. Can you name another food that starts with the **Aa** sound?

# Andy's Pictures

Help Andy label his pictures below and on page 69.

**Directions:** Trace the words. Then, say the words aloud. Listen to the sound that **Aa** makes.

## One Step Further

Draw something else that Andy might have a picture of.

## One Step Further
Name as many words as you can that start with the **Aa** sound.

# "Egg-ceptional" E!

**Directions:** Draw a line from each egg to a picture that begins with the sound of **Ee**. Draw an **X** on the picture that does **not** belong.

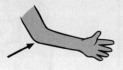

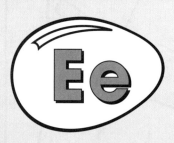

## One Step Further

What is your favorite breakfast food?
Does it start with the **Ee** sound?

# In Elmo's Room

Below and on page 72 are some things that are in Elmo's room.

**Directions:** Trace the words. Then, say the words aloud. Listen to the sound that **Ee** makes.

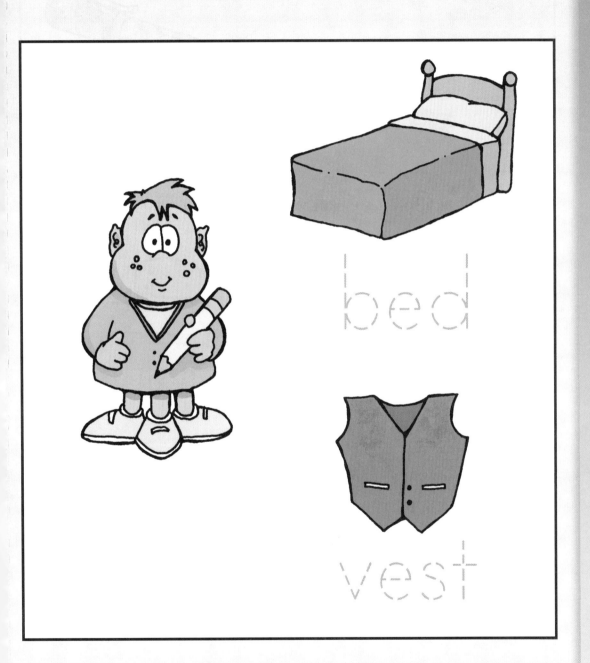

bed

vest

### One Step Further
Look around your room for objects that have the **Ee** sound.

# In Elmo's Room

pen

desk

## One Step Further
Sit at a desk at home or school and write a
letter to a friend.

# Make a Wish

The monsters are at a wishing well. Find out what each one is hoping to get.

**Directions:** Write **i** on the lines to complete each word. Then, say the words aloud.

p___g

m___tt

f___sh

d___sh

## One Step Further

Pretend you are at a wishing well.
What would you wish for?

# Izzy's Gifts

Look at Izzy's birthday gifts! Help her label them.

**Directions:** Trace the words below and on page 75. Then, say the words aloud. Listen to the sound that **Ii** makes.

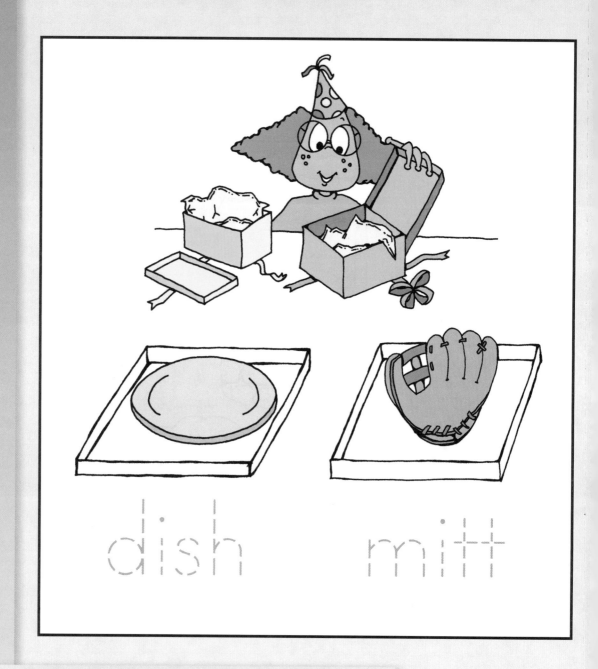

dish          mitt

## One Step Further

Grab a mitt and play catch with a friend.
How many times did you catch the ball?

Kindergarten Essentials

# Izzy's Gifts

pig     fish

## One Step Further
What gifts do you want to give a friend for his or her next birthday?

READING

# Oo Animal Search

Can you find the **Oo** animals?

**Directions:** Trace each **Oo**. Color the animals that begin with the sound of **Oo**.

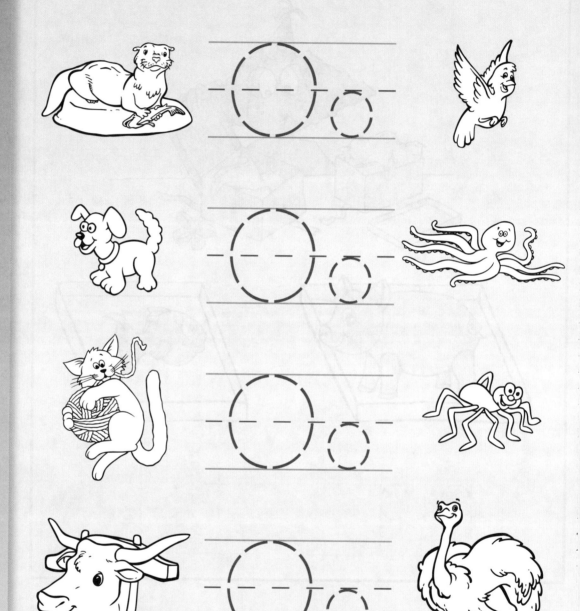

## One Step Further

Choose an animal that you colored on this page. Where might you find this animal?

# Olive's Box

What things are in Olive's box?

**Directions:** Trace the words below and on page 78. Then, say the words aloud. Listen to the sound that **Oo** makes.

sock     clock

**One Step Further**
Look around your home for a sock and a clock. Where did you find these objects?

# Olive's Box

top          doll

## One Step Further
Work with a friend to name as many words
with the **Oo** sound as you can.

# Unusual Umbrellas

**Directions:** Draw a line from each child to a picture that begins with the sound of **Uu**.

**READING**

### One Step Further
Pretend it's raining and stand under an umbrella.

Kindergarten Essentials

# Ug's Puppets

Ug collects puppets. Some of his puppets are shown below and on page 81.

**Directions:** Trace the words. Then, say the words aloud. Listen to the sound that **Uu** makes.

bug          cub

## One Step Further

Ask an adult to help make a puppet of your own. Put on a puppet show!

# Ug's Puppets

duck

pup

READING

**One Step Further**
Tell a story about a pup and a duck.
Make puppets if you want!

# Animal Snapshots

**Directions:** Write **a**, **e**, **i**, **o**, or **u** on each line.

p____g       c____t       b____t

h____n       ____nt       f____sh

d____g       fr____g       d____ck

## One Step Further

Ask a friend to name more animals.
What vowels do those words contain?

Kindergarten Essentials

# Strawberry Patch Match

**Directions:** Draw a line from each uppercase letter to its lowercase letter.

**One Step Further**
What is your favorite fruit? What is your least favorite fruit?

# See the Shells

**Directions:** Draw a line from each uppercase letter to its lowercase letter.

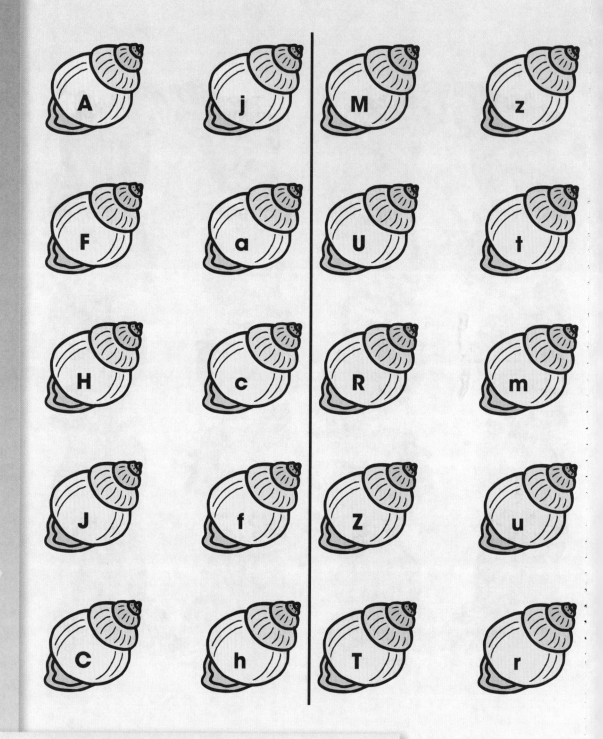

A   j   M   z

F   a   U   t

H   c   R   m

J   f   Z   u

C   h   T   r

## One Step Further

Some people collect seashells. What do you collect?

Kindergarten Essentials

# Haystack Match

**Directions:** Draw a line from each uppercase letter to its lowercase letter.

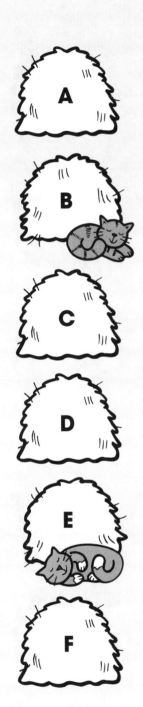

READING

## One Step Further
What do you think the phrase "Needle in a haystack" means?

# Make a Match

**Directions:** Draw a line from each uppercase letter to its lowercase letter.

## One Step Further

Why does your name always start with an uppercase letter?

# A Long Time Ago

**Directions:** Color the picture. Then, trace the words below.

**READING**

dinosaurs

trees grass

## One Step Further
Have you ever seen a real dinosaur? Why or why not?

# Tractor Pull

**Directions:** Color the picture of the farm. Then, trace the words below.

farmer cow

tractor corn

## One Step Further
Would you like to work on a farm? Why or why not?

# Building a House

**Directions:** Color the picture. Then, trace the words below.

wood house

tools work

### One Step Further
Tell a story about a time that you worked hard for something.

# You've Arrived!

**Directions:** Color the picture. Then, trace the words below.

## Welcome
## to the zoo.

## One Step Further

What are your top five favorite animals to see at the zoo?

# Under the Sea

**Directions:** Find the word in each row. Color the boxes to show the word.

| crab | v | c | r | a | b |
| whale | w | h | a | l | e |
| seal | s | e | a | l | t |
| shark | s | h | a | r | k |
| clam | r | c | l | a | m |

READING

## One Step Further
Make a word search using the words on this page. See if a friend can solve it.

Kindergarten Essentials

# Words That Go

**Directions:** Find the word in each row. Color the boxcs to show the word.

| | | | | | |
|---|---|---|---|---|---|
| t | r | a | i | n | j |
| c | b | u | s | a | b |
| f | e | r | r | y | t |
| d | m | j | e | t | b |
| c | a | n | o | e | m |

train

bus

ferry

jet

canoe

## One Step Further

What is your favorite way to travel? How many times have you traveled that way?

# In the Garden

**Directions:** Find the word in each row. Color the boxes to show the word.

| a | b | e | e | g | h |
| f | l | o | w | e | r |
| r | f | t | r | e | e |
| r | a | b | b | i | t |
| s | n | a | i | l | z |

bee

flower

tree

rabbit

snail

READING

## One Step Further
Name two more things you might find in a garden.

Kindergarten Essentials

# Building Words

**Directions:** Find the word in each row. Color the boxes to show the word.

| | | | | | |
|---|---|---|---|---|---|
| t | d | s | a | w | b |
| b | n | a | i | l | y |
| i | h | w | o | o | d |
| e | t | r | u | c | k |
| d | r | i | l | l | a |
| f | r | o | o | f | m |

saw

nail

wood

truck

drill

roof

## One Step Further

Name something else that goes with the objects on this page.

READING

# People

**Directions:** Draw a line to match each word with its picture.

boy

girl

man

woman

**One Step Further**
Name a person you know that fits in each of the categories on this page.

# Things

**Directions:** Draw a line to match each word with its picture.

## ball

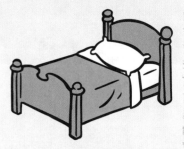

## apple

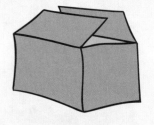

## bed

## box

### One Step Further
Look around your home.
Can you find a ball, apple, bed, and box?

Kindergarten Essentials

# Action Words

**Directions:** Draw a line to match the action word with the person doing that action.

walk

run

talk

eat

**READING**

### One Step Further
Show how you can do each of the action words on this page.

# Action Words

**Directions:** Draw a line to match the action word with the person doing that action.

play

ride

sit

cook

## One Step Further

What is your favorite thing to do after school—play, ride, sit, or cook?

# Descriptions

**Directions:** Draw a line to match each word with its picture.

tall

short

old

big

**One Step Further**
Name an object that fits each of the description words on this page.

# Descriptions

**Directions:** Draw a line to match each word with its picture.

little

happy

sad

funny

## One Step Further

Name something that makes you happy.
Name something you think is funny.

# Which Items Do You Not Need?

Lauren and her dad want to play tennis.

**Directions:** Draw an **X** on the things they do **not** need to play tennis.

**READING**

**One Step Further**
What things do you need to play your favorite sport?

# Which Items Do You Not Need?

Lloyd is working at a bakery.

**Directions:** Draw an **X** on the things he will **not** need to do his job well.

## One Step Further
What might Lloyd be baking today?
Do you like to bake?

Kindergarten Essentials

# Which Picture Is Missing?

**Directions:** Look at the pictures below. They start to make a story, but the last box is empty.

**Directions:** Which of these pictures helps to finish the story? Circle the picture.

## One Step Further

Tell a story about what is happening in the picture. Where is the family driving to?

Kindergarten Essentials

# Which Picture Is Missing?

**Directions:** Look at the pictures below. They start to make a story, but the last box is empty.

**Directions:** Which of these pictures helps to finish the story? Circle the picture.

**One Step Further**
On a warm day, have a water balloon toss with a friend.

# Rainbow Clues

**Directions:** Follow the clues below. Circle your choices.

Find the object that is **brown** and **hard**.

Find the object that is yellow and **long**.

Find the object that is **blue** and **tiny**.

**One Step Further**

Choose an object on this page. Give a friend two clues that describe the object.

# Color It Again

**Directions:** Color the picture in each row that both words describe.

**round** and **orange**

**scared** and **brown**

**wet** and **pointy**

## One Step Further
Find an object in your school that is big and brown. What did you find?

Kindergarten Essentials

# Grandma Gertie

Grandma Gertie loves flowers.

**Directions:** Use the clues below to find the perfect flower for Grandma. Circle your answer.

Grandma likes flowers that are **pink**.
She likes flowers that are tall.
She likes flowers that come with candy.

**One Step Further**
What do you think makes the perfect flower?
Draw it and give it to a friend.

READING

# Jalen's Vacation

Jalen wants to go on vacation. Help him pick out the best spot for his trip.

**Directions:** Read the clues below. Circle the trip that Jalen should pick.

Jalen does not want to go to a cold place.
Jalen does not want to go to a beach.
Jalen wants to go to a place with games.

## One Step Further

Where would you most like to go on vacation? What would you do there?

# A Busy Day

We always get up early. Dad makes us breakfast. I feed Zip, the cat. Then, I walk to school. Mom and Dad go to work.

**Directions:** Read the story. Answer the questions.

What words from the story begin with the same sound as ?

_____

- - - - - - - - - - - - - - - - - - - - - - - - -

_____

Circle the picture that rhymes with **walk**.

Which word in the story means **Mom**, **Dad**, and **I** together?

_____

- - - - - - - - - - - - - - - - - - - - - - - - -

_____

Why does everyone get up early?

_____

- - - - - - - - - - - - - - - - - - - - - - - - -

_____

**One Step Further**
What do you do before school?
What time do you get up in the morning?

# The Goat

On Saturday, Grandma and I went bike riding. Grandma wore her straw hat. We rode along the bike path to the high school. We went to the farm animal show. We got to pet the goats. Grandma left her hat on the bike seat. A goat ate the hat!

**Directions:** Read the story. Answer the questions.

Circle the picture that has the sound of **e** in **pet**.

Circle the picture that names a word that rhymes with **goat**.

Which word in the story is a day of the week?

_ _ _ _ _ _ _ _ _ _ _ _ _ _ _ _

Where does the bike path go?

_ _ _ _ _ _ _ _ _ _ _ _ _ _ _ _

### One Step Further
Where is your favorite place to ride your bike? Is there a bike path near your home?

# Antarctic Penguins

Penguins are birds but they don't fly. Penguins swim. Penguins lay eggs. Most penguin chicks have fluffy feathers. Penguins live in large groups.

**Directions:** Read the story. Answer the questions.

Circle the picture whose name begins with the blend you hear at the beginning of **fluffy**.

What word from the story rhymes with **legs**?

_____

_____

What word from the story means the same as **do not**?

_____

_____

Do all birds fly?

_____

_____

## One Step Further
Where do penguins live?
Have you ever seen a penguin?

READING

Kindergarten Essentials

# Bear Cubs

Bear cubs are born in winter. They may weigh less than a pound. In spring, the cubs and their mother go outside. Their mother teaches them how to find food. The cubs stay with their mother for a year or two. Then, the cubs go out on their own.

**Directions:** Read the story. Answer the questions.

Circle the picture that begins with the blend you hear at the beginning of **grow**.

What words in the story rhyme with **day**?

_____

_ _ _ _ _ _ _ _ _ _ _ _ _ _ _ _

What word in the story means **a cold time of the year**?

_____

_ _ _ _ _ _ _ _ _ _ _ _ _ _ _ _

Why do you think the cubs stay with their mother for a year or two?

_____

_ _ _ _ _ _ _ _ _ _ _ _ _ _ _ _

_____

**One Step Further**
Name a place where you might see a bear cub. Have you ever seen a bear cub?

# Math

MATH

# Zero 0

**Directions:** Circle the number of fish in each tank.

0     1     3          0     1     2

3     4     5          0     1     2

0     1     2          1     2     4

## One Step Further

How many fish do you own? Draw a
picture of the biggest fish you've seen.

# One 1

**Directions:** Trace the big **1**. Color the pictures.

115

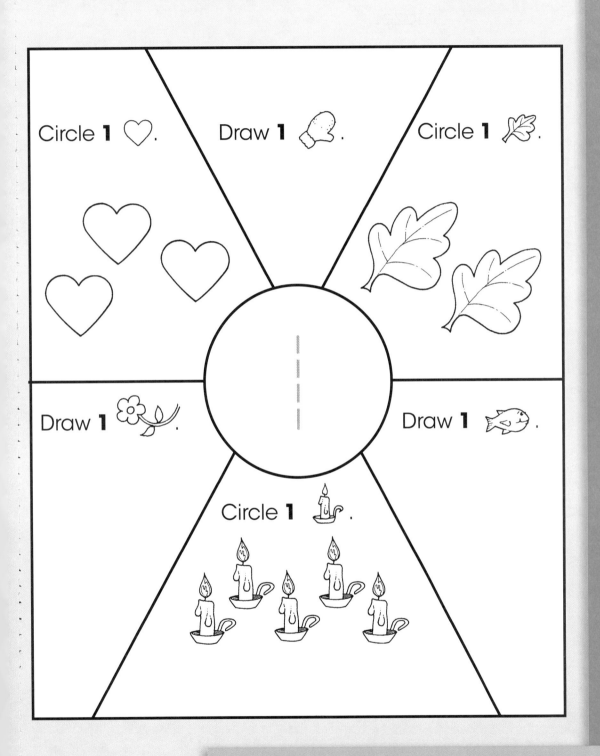

**MATH**

### One Step Further
Name something in your kitchen you see one of. What do you use that object for?

_navigation">Kindergarten Essentials

# Two 2

**Directions:** Help the bunny twins catch their balloons. Follow the twos through the maze.

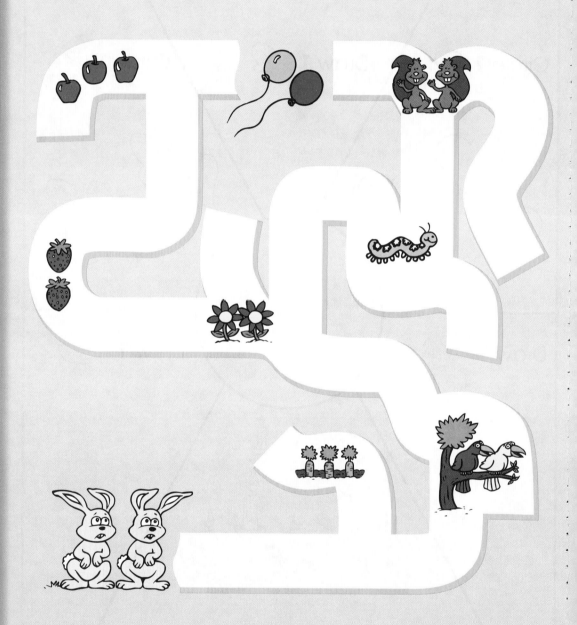

## One Step Further
Look around your neighborhood.
Name something you see two of.

# Three 3

**Directions:** Count and write the number in each box. Circle the groups of three. Color the groups of four.

**One Step Further**
Name three more fruits.
Which is your favorite?

# Four 4

**Directions:** Color to find the hidden picture.

**2** = blue      **3** = blue      **4** = green

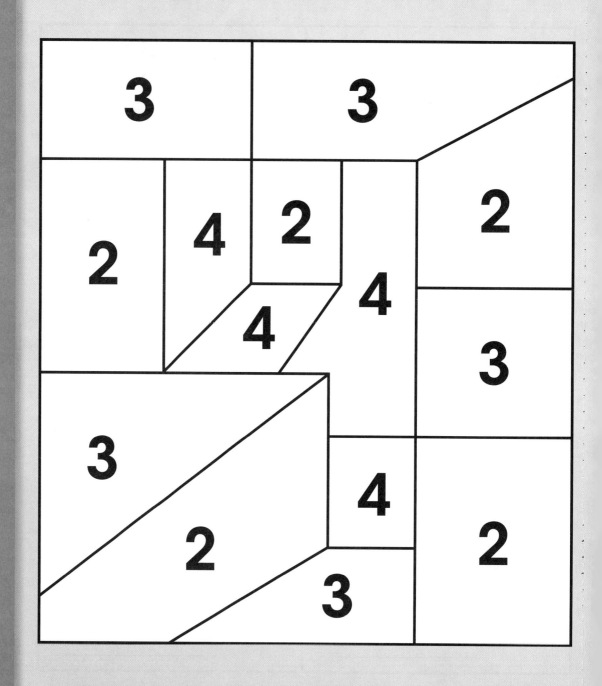

MATH

## One Step Further
Name four objects that go together.
Are all those objects the same color?

# Five 5

**Directions:** Five dogs are colored. Color five dogs.

MATH

## One Step Further
Pretend you are a dog. Bark five times.
Name the five dogs you colored.

# Review Numbers 0-5

**Directions:** Connect the dots in order. Color the picture.

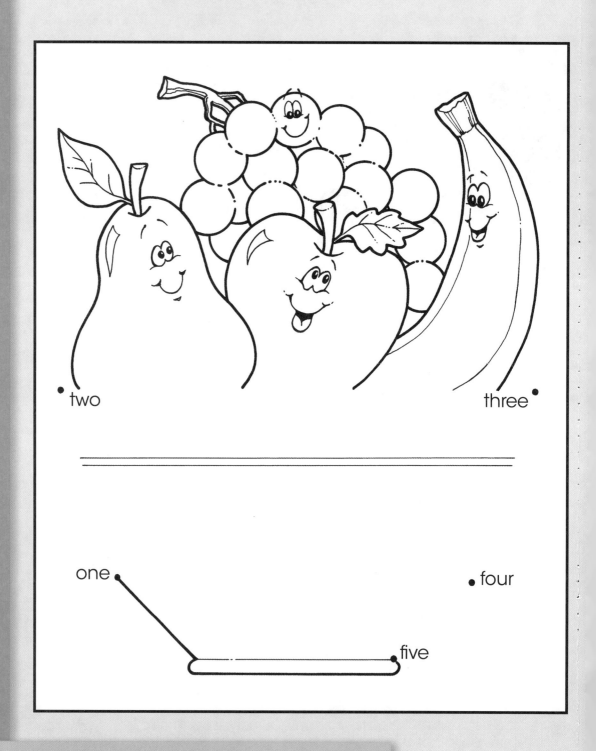

two

three

one

four

five

## One Step Further

Find five of your favorite books.
Ask an adult to read to you.

# Six 6

**Directions:** Count and color each picture. Circle each group of six.

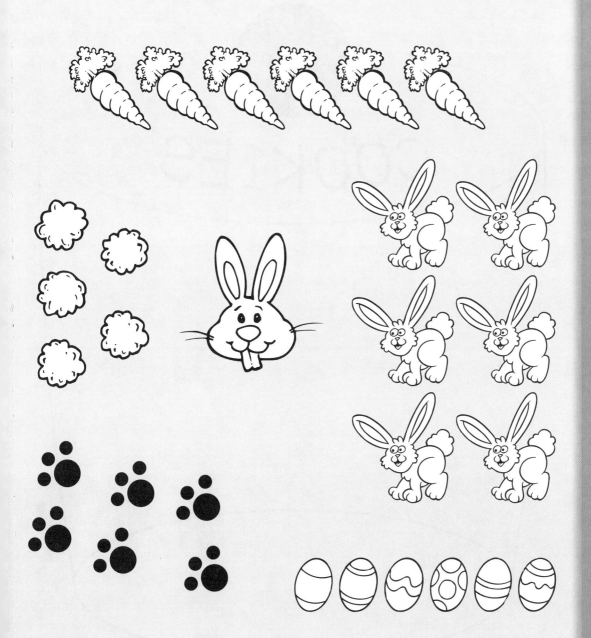

## One Step Further

Hop like a bunny six times.
For your next snack, eat six baby carrots.

# Seven 7

**Directions:** Draw seven cookies.

## One Step Further
Some people think seven is a lucky number.
What is your lucky number?

# Eight 8

**Directions:** Count and color eight pieces of gold in each of the treasure chests. Then, color the treasure chests.

**MATH**

## One Step Further

Name other things you might find in a treasure chest.

# Nine 9

**Directions:** Draw nine s in the . Color the s.

MATH

## One Step Further
Put a handful of jellybeans in a jar.
Ask a friend to guess how many are in the jar.

# Ten 10

**Directions:** Color five dots **red**, three dots **blue**, and two dots **orange** on the butterfly. Count the dots on the butterfly.

How many are there altogether? _____

**One Step Further**
Draw a picture of the prettiest butterfly you've seen.

# Review Numbers 0-10

**Directions:** Count the beads in each row. Write the number.

_____

– – – –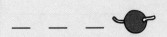

_____

– – – –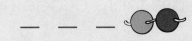

_____
_____

– – – –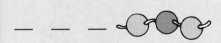

_____

– – – –

_____

– – – –

_____

– – – –

_____

– – – –

_____

– – – –

_____

– – – –

_____
_____

– – – –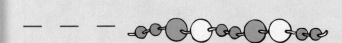

_____

## One Step Further

Find several small objects. Separate them into 10 piles. How many are in each pile?

Kindergarten Essentials

# Numbers 1-10

**Directions:** Circle the words in the puzzle. The words go across and down.

```
w t t o n e r s
n w t h r e e f
i o u s i x q i
n v e i g h t v
e f o u r b e e
x s e v e n n o
```

| | | | |
|---|---|---|---|
| **1** | one | **2** | two |
| **3** | three | **4** | four |
| **5** | five | **6** | six |
| **7** | seven | **8** | eight |
| **9** | nine | **10** | ten |

## One Step Further
Look for loose change around your home. Make **10** piles of **10** coins each.

Kindergarten Essentials

# A Dinosaur Dig

**Directions:** Find **7** shovels below and color them. Then, color the rest of the picture.

MATH

## One Step Further

Would you want to go on a dig for dinosaur bones? Why or why not?

# A Nest of Eggs

**Directions:** Count the eggs in each nest. Write the number on the line.

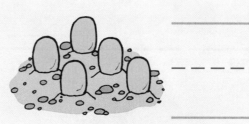

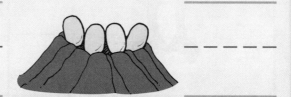

**MATH**

## One Step Further

What animals might be inside the eggs on this page?

Kindergarten Essentials

# Perfect Peacocks

**Directions:** Count the number of feathers on each peacock. Write the number on the line.

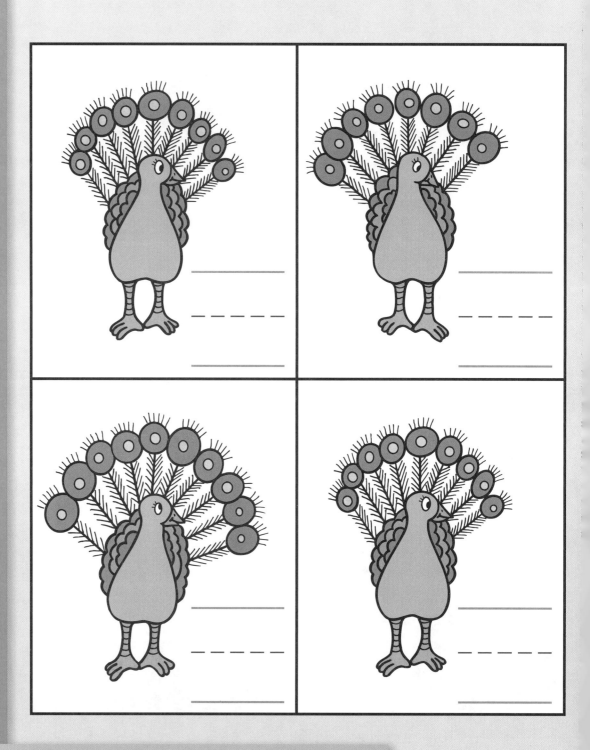

## One Step Further
Feathers come in all sorts of colors. Draw and color a feather however you want!

MATH

# Missing Numbers

**Directions:** Write the missing number in each box.

| 1 | | 3 |
|---|---|---|

| 8 | | 10 |
|---|---|---|

| 6 | | 8 |
|---|---|---|

**MATH**

### One Step Further
Create your own missing number problems.
See how many a friend can get right.

# Trace and Write 11

**Directions:** Trace and write the number **11**. Then, count and write the numbers.

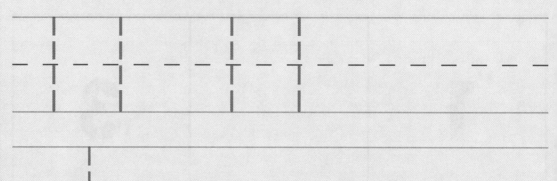

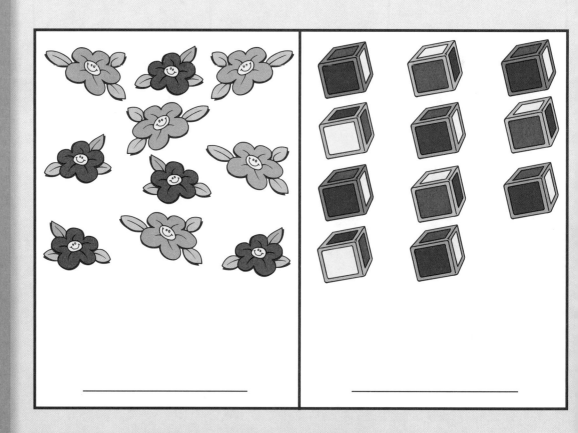

### One Step Further

Look around your neighborhood for 11 flowers. Where did you find them?

# Eleven 11

**Directions:** Count Zeb Zebra's stripes and color them.

MATH

**One Step Further**
Draw a zoo animal that has spots.
Draw 11 spots on the animal.

# Trace and Write 12

**Directions:** Trace and write the number **12**. Then, count and write the numbers.

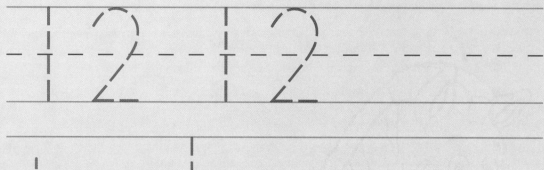

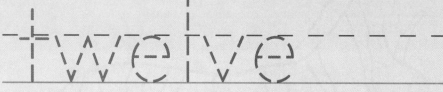

**MATH**

_____          _____

## One Step Further
How many balls can you find in your school?
What do you like to do on the playground?

# Twelve 12

**Directions:** Count each group of creatures. Draw a line from the creatures to their matching apples.

**MATH**

## One Step Further
Sit outside for awhile. How many birds do you see? How many butterflies do you see?

# Trace and Write 13

**Directions:** Trace and write the number **13** and the number word.

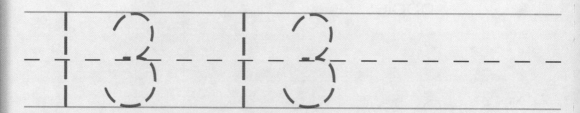

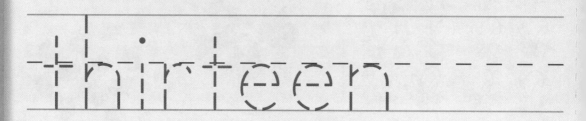

**Directions:** Now practice writing the number and the word by yourself on the lines below.

## One Step Further

How many letters are in your first name?
How many letters are in your last name?

# Thirteen 13

**Directions:** Color the number. Color the word. Count and color the rest of the picture.

## One Step Further

Look at the front lawn of your home or school. Name 13 things you see.

Kindergarten Essentials

# Trace and Write 14

**Directions:** Trace and write the number **14** and the number word.

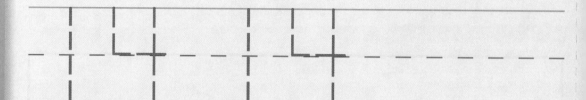

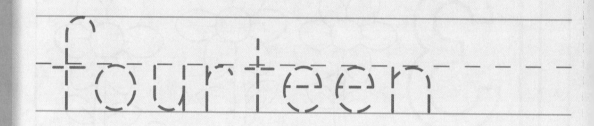

**Directions:** Now practice writing the number and the word by yourself on the lines below.

**MATH**

## One Step Further

Look around your home.
Find 14 black objects. What did you find?

# Fourteen 14

**Directions:** Color the number. Color the word. Count and color the rest of the picture.

### One Step Further
Name as many beverages as you can.
Can you name 14?

# Trace and Write 15

**Directions:** Trace and write the number **15** and the
number word.

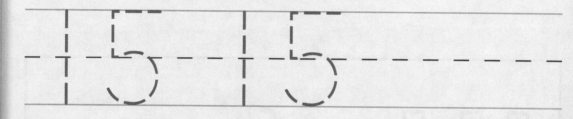

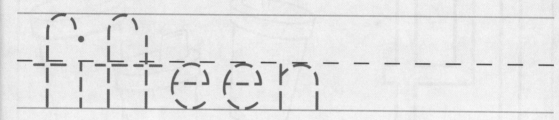

**Directions:** Now practice writing the number and
the word by yourself on the lines below.

**MATH**

## One Step Further
Read a book for 15 minutes.
Ask an adult to help you.

# Fifteen 15

**Directions:** Color the number. Color the word. Count and color the rest of the picture.

MATH

## One Step Further

What is your favorite thing to do in the summer?

Kindergarten Essentials

# Trace and Write 16

**Directions:** Trace and write the number **16** and the number word.

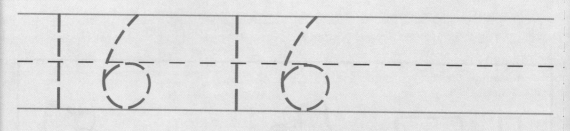

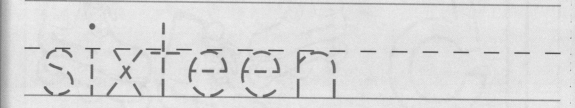

**Directions:** Now practice writing the number and the word by yourself on the lines below.

**MATH**

## One Step Further
Tell a story about your favorite birthday.
How old were you? How old are you now?

# Sixteen 16

**Directions:** Color the number. Color the word. Count and color the rest of the picture.

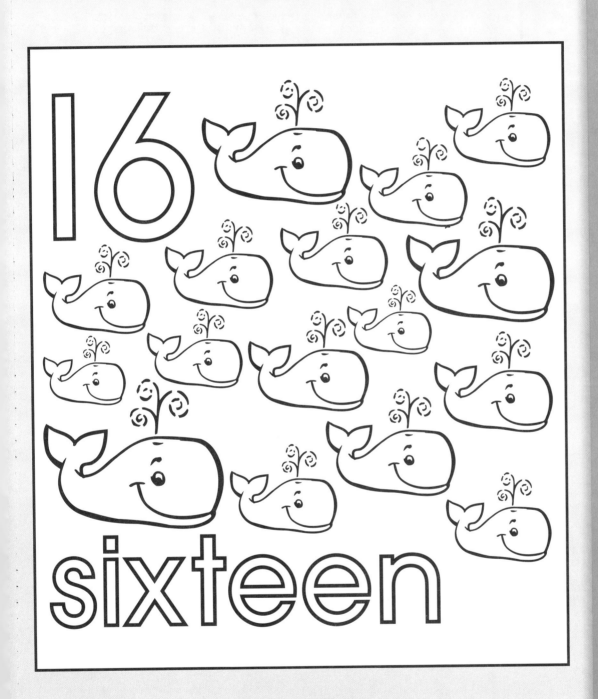

MATH

**One Step Further**
Name other things you might see in the ocean. How many can you name?

# Trace and Write 17

**Directions:** Trace and write the number **17** and the number word.

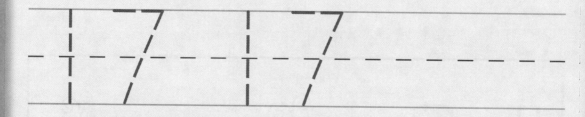

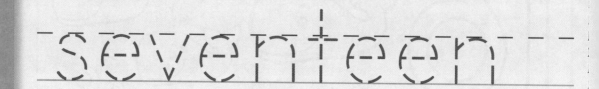

**Directions:** Now practice writing the number and the word by yourself on the lines below.

**MATH**

## One Step Further

Look around your room and count 17 small objects.

# Seventeen 17

**Directions:** Color the number. Color the word. Count and color the rest of the picture.

## One Step Further

Name things you use to get ready for school. How many can you name?

# Trace and Write 18

**Directions:** Trace and write the number **18** and the number word.

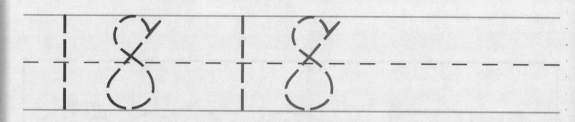

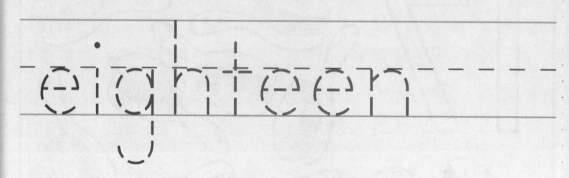

**Directions:** Now practice writing the number and the word by yourself on the lines below.

## One Step Further

What can you grow in a garden?
See how many things you can name.

# Eighteen 18

**Directions:** Color the number. Color the word. Count and color the rest of the picture.

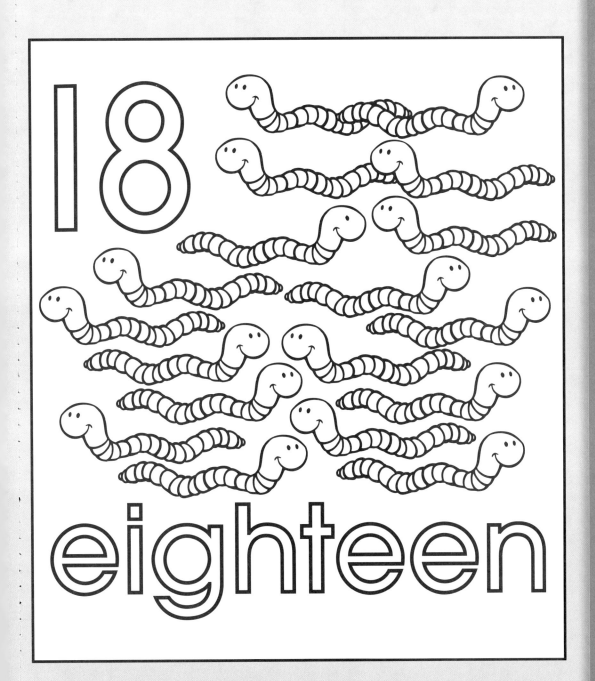

**One Step Further**
Describe a worm to a friend.
Tell a story about the worm.

# Trace and Write 19

**Directions:** Trace and write the number **19** and the number word.

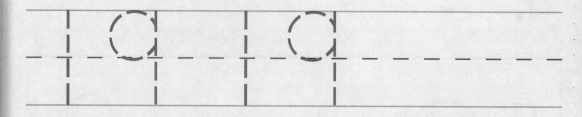

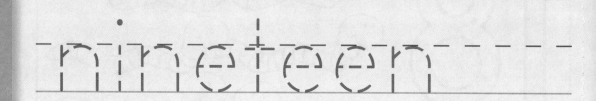

**Directions:** Now practice writing the number and the word by yourself on the lines below.

## One Step Further

What animals make good pets?
See how many you can name.

# Nineteen 19

**Directions:** Color the number. Color the word. Count and color the rest of the picture.

**One Step Further**
Name the fish in this picture.
Where do you think the fish are swimming?

# Trace and Write 20

**Directions:** Trace and write the number **20** and the number word.

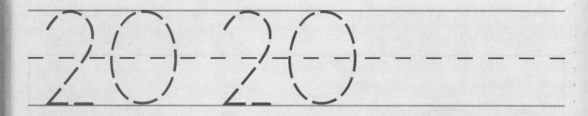

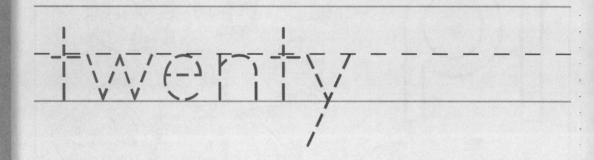

**Directions:** Now practice writing the number and the word by yourself on the lines below.

MATH

## One Step Further
Find 20 pebbles outside your home or school.
Which one is the biggest?

# Twenty 20

**Directions:** Color the number. Color the word. Count and color the rest of the picture.

**MATH**

**One Step Further**
Find 20 of your favorite objects.
Put them in order from biggest to smallest.

# Review Numbers 0-20

**Directions:** Count the number of colored squares.
Then, write the correct number.

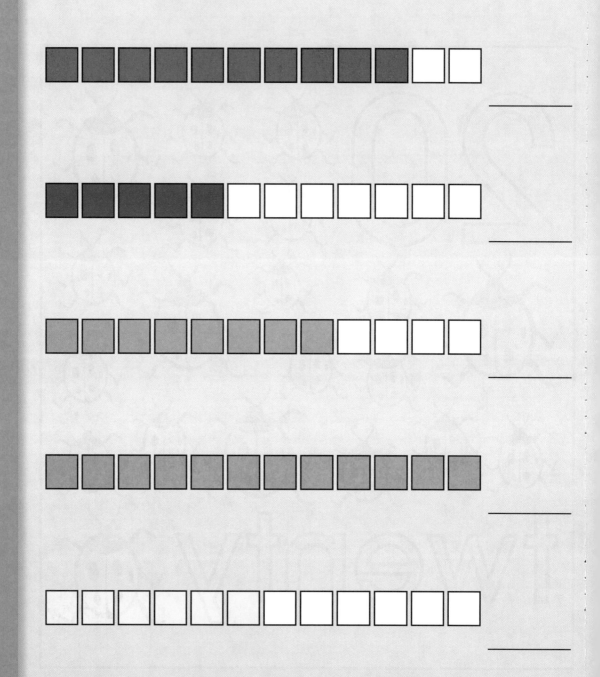

_____

_____

_____

_____

_____

**MATH**

**One Step Further**
There are five purple boxes on this page.
Find five purple objects in your home.

# Review Numbers 0-20

**Directions:** Count the number of colored squares.
Then, write the correct number.

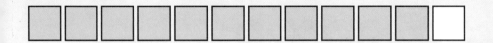

_____

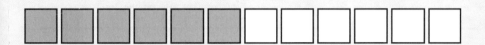

_____

_____

_____

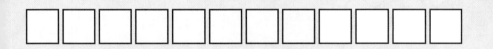

_____

MATH

## One Step Further

Name something that you own six of.
Find six orange objects at school.

Kindergarten Essentials

# Review Numbers 0-20

**Directions:** Count the first row of beads. Circle the next row of beads to show that it has more than **10** beads. Circle the rows of beads with more than **10**.

## One Step Further

Find as many crayons as you can.
How many did you find?

# Review Numbers 0-20

**Directions:** Connect the dots in order from **1** to **20**.
Color the surprise!

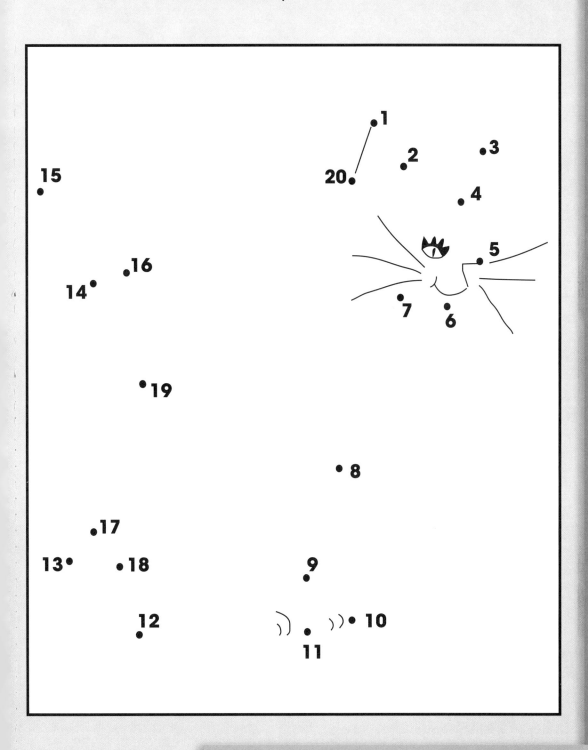

**MATH**

## One Step Further

Look out the window.
Count the cars you see until you get to 20.

Kindergarten Essentials

# Happy Hippo

**Directions:** Write the missing numbers. Color the picture.

| 1 | __ | 3 | __ | 5 |
|---|----|----|----|----|
| 6 | 7 | __ | __ | __ |
| 11 | __ | 13 | __ | __ |
| __ | 17 | __ | __ | 20 |

## One Step Further

Count to **20** as fast as you can. Ask an adult to time you.

# Spotty Leopards

**Directions:** Circle the number of spots on each leopard.

**17    18    19**

**17    18    19**

**17    18    19**

**17    18    19**

MATH

## One Step Further

Draw another animal that has spots. Draw **19** spots on the animal.

# A Super Sea Turtle

**Directions:** Connect the dots from **1** to **20**. Color the picture.

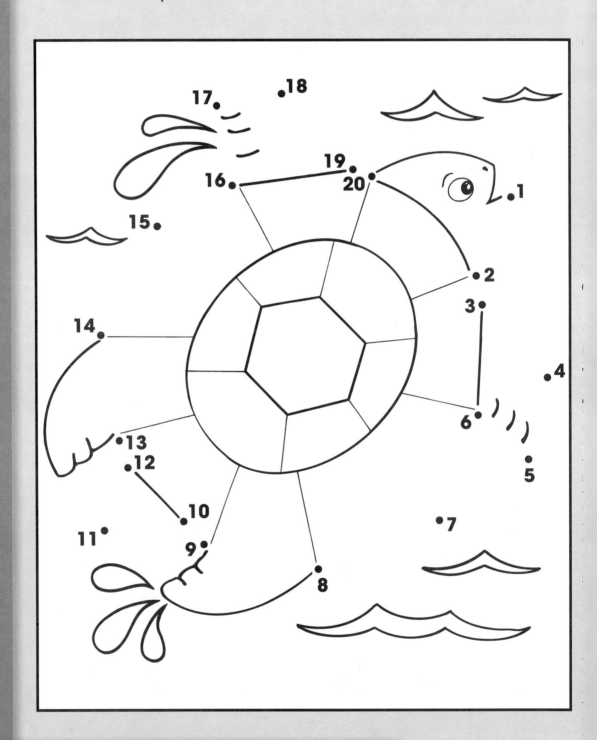

## One Step Further

Turtles walk slowly. Walk slowly around a table or desk.

# Time to Sleep

**Directions:** Connect the dots from **1** to **20**. Color the picture.

**MATH**

## One Step Further

What is your favorite activity to do with an adult?

# Elephant Snacks

**Directions:** Count the peanuts in each bag. Then, write the number on the line.

## One Step Further
Count the peanuts on this page. How many peanuts can each elephant eat?

# Feeding the Birds

**Directions:** Draw **15** more pieces of birdseed in the bag. Then, answer the question below.

How many pieces of birdseed are in the bag now? _____

## One Step Further

With an adult, make a bird feeder. Fill it with birdseed and put it outside your home.

# Most

**Directions:** Color the pictures in the box that has the **most** candy.

MATH

## One Step Further
Give a friend some strawberries and keep some for yourself. Who has the most?

# Fewest

**Directions:** Color the pictures in the box that has the **fewest** bugs.

MATH

## One Step Further

Count your socks and your shirts. Which do you have the fewest of?

Kindergarten Essentials

# Thinking Skills

**Directions:** Read the clues below. Draw an **X** on the numbers that do not fit the clues. Circle the correct number.

The number is greater than 1.
The number is less than 6.
The number is not 2.

MATH

7          5

2          0

## One Step Further

Think of a number. Give clues to a friend to help him or her guess the correct number.

# Thinking Skills

**Directions:** Read the clues below. Draw an **X** on the numbers that do not fit the clues. Circle the correct number.

The number is less than 7.
The number is greater than 2.
The number equals 3 + 1.

8

3

4

1

MATH

### One Step Further
Think of an object. What clues would lead a friend to guess what you're thinking of?

# All Aboard!

**Directions:** Count the windows on each car to solve the problem. Write the answer under the last car.

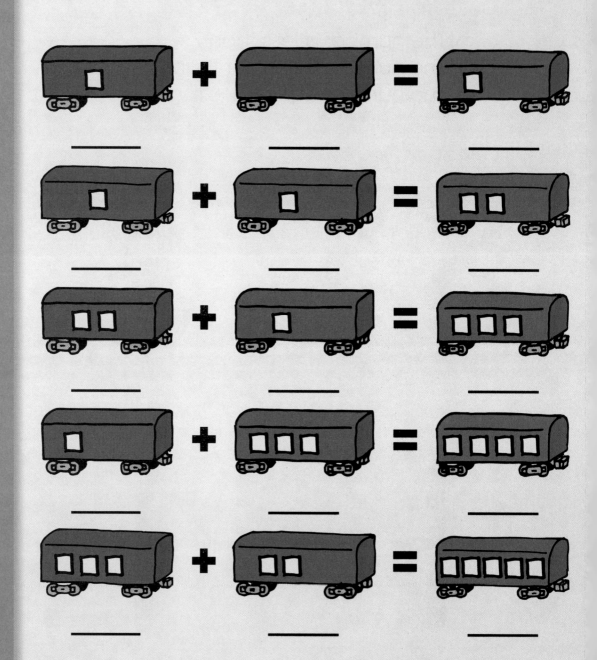

## One Step Further

How many words can you name that rhyme with **train**?

# Mmmm...Pie

**Directions:** Solve each problem. Write the answer on the pie.

2 + 2 = ____

4 + 2 = ____

1 + 0 = ____

3 + 2 = ____

2 + 1 = ____

1 + 1 = ____

**MATH**

**Riddle:** What should we give during harvest time?

**Directions:** To find the answer, write the letter from each pie on the correct line below.

___ ___ ___ ___ ___ ___
6   3   1   5   2   4

**One Step Further**
How many different kinds of pie can you name?

# Monkeys Love Bananas!

**Directions:** Solve each problem. Write the answer on the line.

$2 + 1 =$ _____

$1 + 3 =$ _____

$1 + 1 =$ _____

$3 + 2 =$ _____

$4 + 1 =$ _____

$1 + 0 =$ _____

## One Step Further
Bananas are a monkey's favorite fruit. What is your favorite fruit?

# Graphing

**Directions:** Count the shapes in the picture. Then, color the graph below.

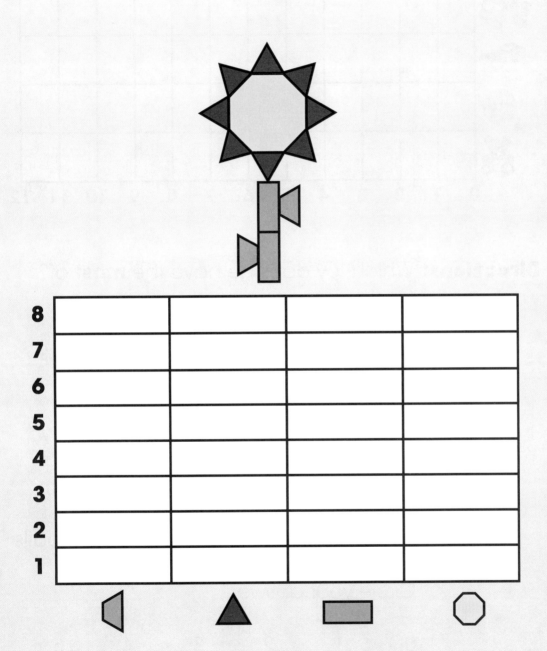

| | | | |
|---|---|---|---|
| 8 | | | |
| 7 | | | |
| 6 | | | |
| 5 | | | |
| 4 | | | |
| 3 | | | |
| 2 | | | |
| 1 | | | |

MATH

## One Step Further

What other pictures can you draw using shapes?

# Graphing

John made a chart of some of his toys.

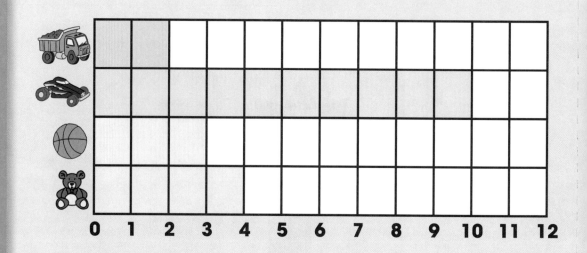

**Directions:** Which toy does he have the **most** of?
Circle your answer.

dump trucks      cars      basketballs      bears

Which toy does he have the **least** of?
Circle your answer.

dump trucks      cars      basketballs      bears

How many more bears than basketballs
does John have?
Circle your answer.

0      1      2      3      4      5

## One Step Further

How many bears do you have?
Do you have more or less than John?

# Garden Friends

**Directions:** Circle the animal that comes next in each row.

## One Step Further

Choose one animal on this page. Tell a story about a day in the life of that animal.

MATH

# Grow a Garden

**Directions:** Circle the item that comes next in each row.

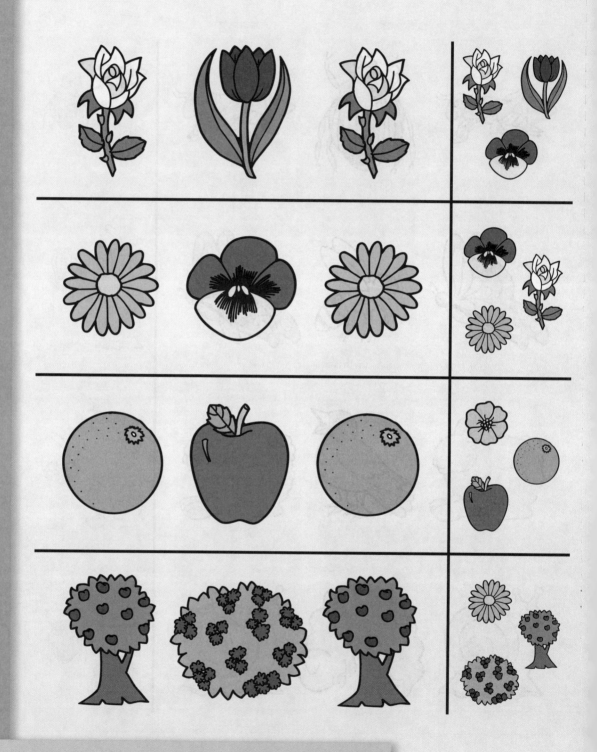

## One Step Further

What can you grow in a garden? See how many things you can name.

MATH

# First

**Directions:** Circle the **first** object in each row.

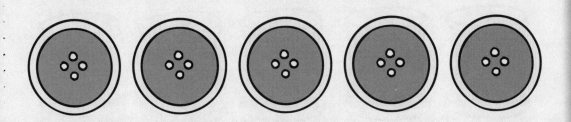

**MATH**

## One Step Further

Tell about a time when you competed at something and came in first.

# Second

**Directions:** Circle the **second** object in each row.

MATH

## One Step Further

Stand in line with three of your friends. Who is second?

**Directions:** Circle the **third** object in each row.

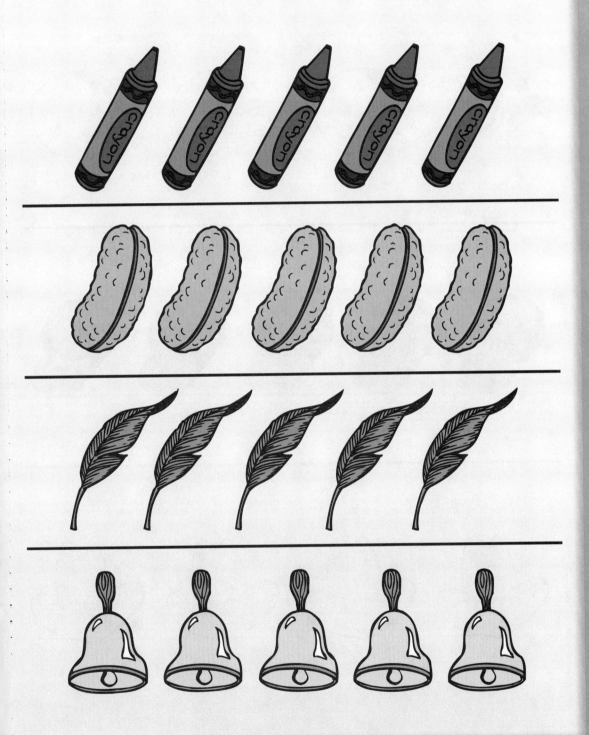

MATH

## One Step Further
Place five of your favorite toys in a line. Which toy is third?

# Fourth

**Directions:** Circle the **fourth** thing in each row.

## One Step Further
Make a list of things to do today.
What is the fourth thing on your list?

# At the Fire Station

**Directions:** Color the squares. Then, color the rest of the picture.

## One Step Further

Look at the outside of your home. How many squares can you find?

# At the Train Yard

**Directions:** Color the rectangles. Then, color the rest of the picture.

**MATH**

## One Step Further

Find a ruler. What shape is the ruler?

# Exploring the Garden

**Directions:** Color the circles and triangles. Then, color the rest of the picture.

MATH

## One Step Further

Draw a triangle and a circle. Then, turn the shapes into drawings of animals.

# Fun on the Farm

**Directions:** Find the circles, triangles, and squares and color them. Then, color the rest of the picture.

MATH

## One Step Further

Imagine you have your very own farm. What would you grow on your farm?

# Games and Activities

# Colors

**Directions:** Circle the words in the puzzle. The words go across and down.

```
b l u e p i n k
b l a c k e r w
r o r a n g e h
o g r e e n d i
w p u r p l e t
n y e l l o w e
```

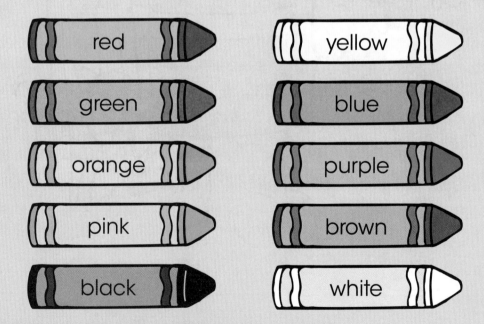

red

yellow

green

blue

orange

purple

pink

brown

black

white

## One Step Further

Choose a color from this page. How many objects can you find that are that color?

# Time for Art

**Directions:** Help Anna find her drawing pad.

## One Step Further
Draw a picture using at least five different colored crayons.

# What Is Round?

**Directions:** Circle the words in the puzzle. The words go across and down.

```
k e a r t h l o
b a l l o m v r
n g l o b e w a
j h u p q r g n
m a r b l e t g
i s m o o n f e
```

 ball

 moon

 globe

 earth

 orange

 marble

## One Step Further

Draw a picture of a circle. Turn the circle into something that is round.

# Swamp Search

**Directions:** Color the circles to get to the swamp.

**GAMES**

## One Step Further
Pretend you are an alligator and use your arms to chomp!

Kindergarten Essentials

# Fun on Skis

**Directions:** Help the skier down the mountain.

## One Step Further
Which activity would you choose: swimming in the summer or skiing in the winter?

# How Is the Weather?

**Directions:** Circle the words in the puzzle. The words go across and down.

| s | w | i | n | d | y | r | c |
|---|---|---|---|---|---|---|---|
| n | d | a | c | b | n | s | l |
| o | e | r | a | i | n | y | o |
| w | q | z | y | o | t | v | u |
| y | w | a | r | m | u | x | d |
| p | s | u | n | n | y | w | y |

 warm

 rainy

 snowy

 windy

 sunny

 cloudy

## One Step Further

What is the weather like today? What is your favorite kind of weather?

Kindergarten Essentials

GAMES

# The Lost Nest

**Directions:** Help the dinosaur mother find her nest of eggs.

## One Step Further

Do you know of any other animals that lay eggs?

# Dino Pet!

**Directions:** If you could have a pet dinosaur, what would it look like? Draw your dinosaur below.

**GAMES**

### One Step Further
Would you like to have a pet dinosaur? Why or why not?

# On the Farm

**Directions:** Circle the words in the puzzle. The words go across and down.

```
p r z h o r s e
q p i g s t j c
t u r k e y u o
n x m y l k w w
o c h i c k e n
s h e e p h v i
```

 pig

 cow

 horse

 sheep

 turkey

 chicken

## One Step Further

Imagine you are on a farm. What might you see when you look around?

GAMES

# Farm Babies

**Directions:** Help the babies find their mothers.

## One Step Further

Name the animals on this page. What are the babies called?

GAMES

Kindergarten Essentials

# A Bone for Skipper

**Directions:** Help Skipper find the bone.

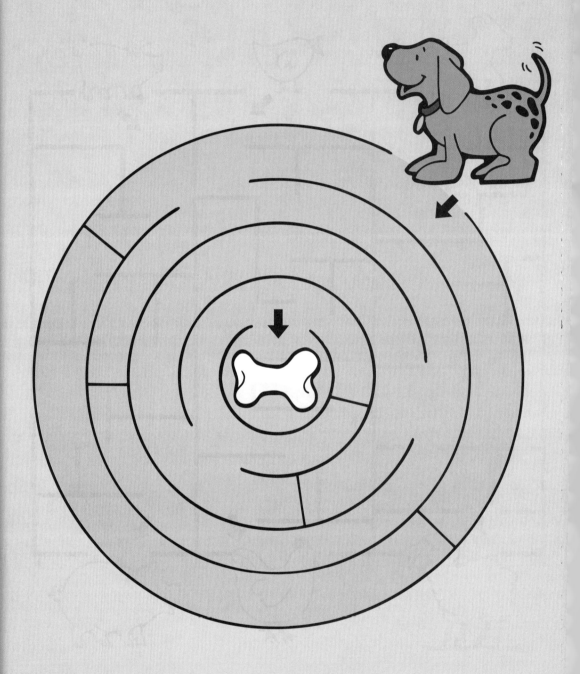

## One Step Further

Design a doghouse for Skipper.

# Pets

**Directions:** Circle the words in the puzzle. The words go across and down.

| r | y | l | i | j | k | h | f |
|---|---|---|---|---|---|---|---|
| a | h | a | m | s | t | e | r |
| b | z | f | i | s | h | c | g |
| b | a | c | a | t | d | u | e |
| i | t | u | r | t | l | e | v |
| t | x | w | m | d | o | g | b |

 cat

 dog

 fish

 hamster

 rabbit

 turtle

## One Step Further

Do you have any pets? What kind of pet would you most like to have?

# A Leafy Path

**Directions:** Help the squirrel find its tree.

## One Step Further
Go outside and make a path of leaves to the nearest tree.

# Forest Babies

**Directions:** Help the babies find their mothers.

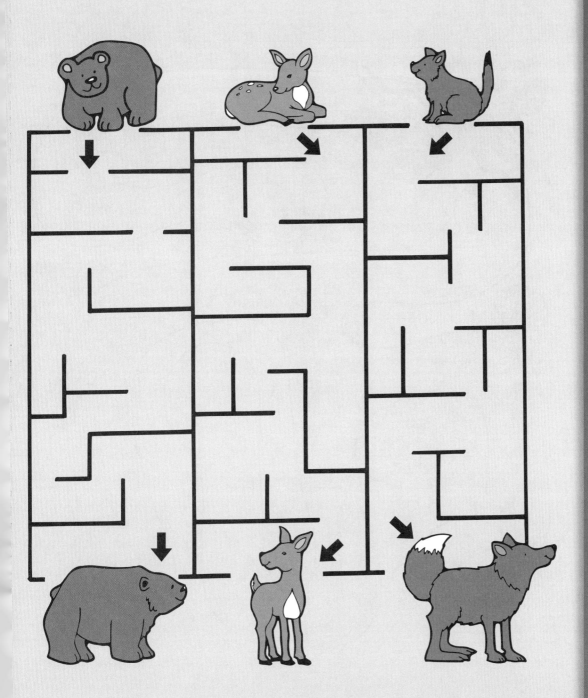

## One Step Further
Tell a story about the animal babies on this page.

# A New Home

**Directions:** Help the hermit crab find a new home.

## One Step Further

Design a shell for the hermit crab to live in.

# In the Ocean

**Directions:** Circle the words in the puzzle. The words go across and down.

```
s  s  u  c  r  a  b  j
h  r  t  v  w  l  k  m
a  d  o  l  p  h  i  n
r  p  w  h  a  l  e  n
k  q  o  i  f  i  s  h
s  e  a  h  o  r  s  e
```

 fish

 crab

 whale

 shark

 dolphin

 seahorse

## One Step Further

Name other things you might see in the ocean. How many can you name?

Kindergarten Essentials

GAMES

# Learning the Past

**Directions:** Help the museum guide find the dinosaur display.

## One Step Further
Do you like going to the museum? What is the most interesting thing you've seen?

# Digging Up Bones

**Directions:** Help the scientist find the dinosaur bones.

## One Step Further
Why do you think dinosaur bones are important?

# School Tools

**Directions:** Circle the words in the puzzle. The words go across and down.

| s | c | i | s | s | o | r | s |
|---|---|---|---|---|---|---|---|
| r | c | r | a | y | o | n | r |
| u | o | u | q | g | l | u | e |
| l | i | x | h | u | g | s | f |
| e | p | e | n | c | i | l | t |
| r | m | z | c | h | a | l | k |

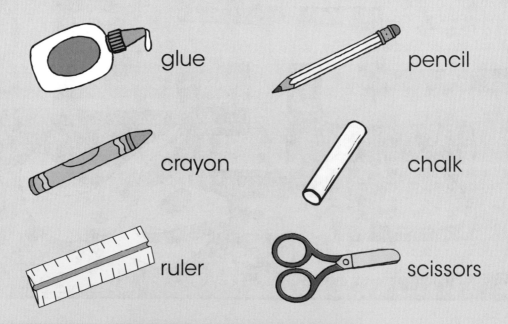

glue

pencil

crayon

chalk

ruler

scissors

## One Step Further
Look at the objects on this page. What else do you need for school?

Kindergarten Essentials

GAMES

# Shapes

**Directions:** Circle the words in the puzzle. The words go across and down.

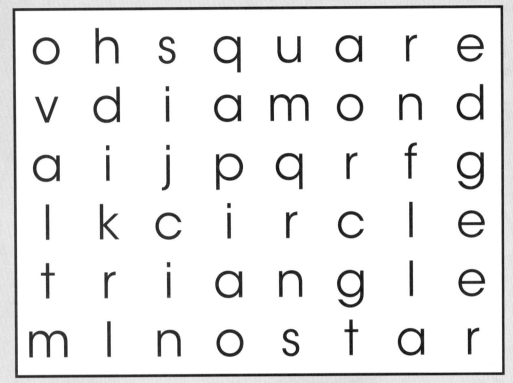

```
o h s q u a r e
v d i a m o n d
a i j p q r f g
l k c i r c l e
t r i a n g l e
m l n o s t a r
```

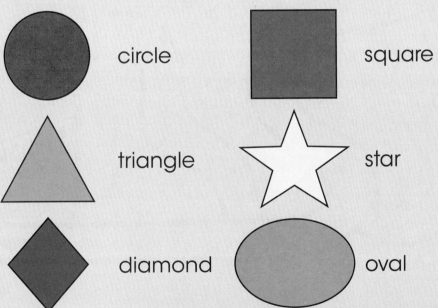

circle     square

triangle     star

diamond     oval

**GAMES**

## One Step Further

Draw a picture of yourself using all the shapes on this page.

# A Speedy Race

**Directions:** Help the race car get to the finish line.

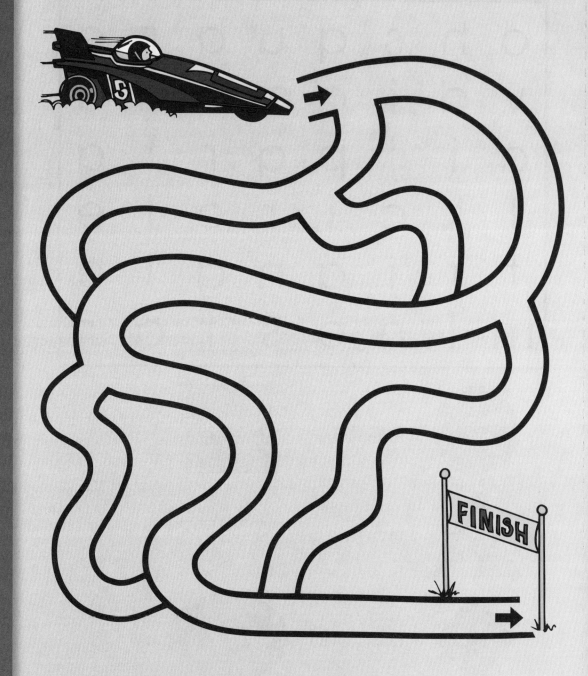

FINISH

## One Step Further
Pretend you are driving a race car. How fast do you go?

# In the Country

**Directions:** Circle the words in the puzzle. The words go across and down.

```
d b z w u v y h
a r f i e l d i
c i x t o w n l
b d p m q e r l
b g r o a d s t
o e m e a d o w
```

 hill

 road

 town

 field

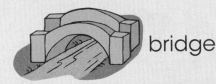 bridge

 meadow

### One Step Further
Create your own word search using words of things you might see in the country.

# Living Things

**Directions:** Circle the words in the puzzle. The words go across and down.

| m | x | c | b | a | b | y | s |
|---|---|---|---|---|---|---|---|
| g | m | a | n | p | b | r | a |
| r | n | o | y | z | q | h | t |
| a | f | l | o | w | e | r | u |
| s | w | d | o | g | v | i | d |
| s | l | k | t | r | e | e | j |

dog

man

tree

baby

grass

flower

## One Step Further

Name three more things that would fit in the "Living Things" category on this page.

GAMES

# Nonliving Things

**Directions:** Circle the words in the puzzle. The words go across and down.

```
g y c l b s k c
c b o o k h m l
a b a l l j t o
r z f a i u n c
d p e n c i l k
e x d o l l v w
```

 car

  doll

 ball

 book

 clock

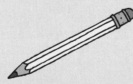 pencil

**GAMES**

### One Step Further

Tell a story that includes at least three of the objects on this page.

Kindergarten Essentials

# Time to Go!

**Directions:** Help the family get home.

## One Step Further

Draw a map of the street you live on. See if a friend can find your home.

# In the City

**Directions:** Circle the words in the puzzle. The words go across and down.

```
t v s t o r e p
a z y j a i g a
x w b c a r h r
i x s c d e f k
h o s p i t a l
u t s t r e e t
```

 car

 park

 taxi

 store

 street

 hospital

**One Step Further**
What are your favorite places to go in the city where you live?

GAMES

Kindergarten Essentials

# Find the Mistakes

**Directions:** Circle **5** mistakes that are in the picture.

## One Step Further

Imagine you wake up one morning and
everything is backward! Tell a story about it.

# On Land

**Directions:** Circle the words in the puzzle. The words go across and down.

```
c a d n c a r s
t b e f k g i j
a v c a m p e r
x a z h b u s t
i n y w l m v u
b i c y c l e x
```

 car

 van

 bus

 taxi

 camper

 bicycle

**GAMES**

### One Step Further
What else can you use to travel? Think big and small!

Kindergarten Essentials

# A Garden Helper

**Directions:** Help the girl find her flower garden.

## One Step Further

How many different types of flowers can you name?

GAMES

# Bugs

**Directions:** Circle the words in the puzzle. The words go across and down.

```
b l a d y b u g
e a k x w n f f
e n y m o t h l
t t z e d u i y
l a b o e b c h
e c r i c k e t
```

 ant

 fly

 moth

 beetle

 ladybug

 cricket

**GAMES**

## One Step Further
Do you like bugs? Why or why not?

# At the Zoo

**Directions:** Circle the words in the puzzle. The words go across and down.

```
s p e a c o c k
e u v y x b z a
a g o r i l l a
l w s t i g e r
e l e p h a n t
t g i r a f f e
```

tiger

seal

giraffe

gorilla

peacock

elephant

## One Step Further

Draw a picture of a day at the zoo. Tell a story about your picture.

GAMES

# Let's Go to the Zoo

**Directions:** Help the family find their way to the zoo.

## One Step Further

Tell a story about a day at the zoo. What animals did you see?

# Community Helpers

**Directions:** Circle the words in the puzzle. The words go across and down.

```
d w d e n t u v
o d e n t i s t
c p l u m b e r
t t n u r s e s
o t e a c h e r
r p a i n t e r
```

 nurse

 teacher

 doctor

 plumber

 dentist

 painter

## One Step Further

What do you want to be when you grow up?
Tell a story about it.

# Money

**Directions:** Circle the words in the puzzle. The words go across and down.

```
g d i m e d p v
d o l l a r e c
n i c k e l n w
s f b e z y n a
u m o n e y y x
t q u a r t e r
```

 money      penny

 nickel      dime

 quarter      dollar

**One Step Further**
Look around your home for all the loose change you can find. Count it.

Kindergarten Essentials

GAMES

# Polar Bear Palace

**Directions:** Circle **6** mistakes that are in the picture.

## One Step Further
If you were a polar bear, what would you do all day?

# A Lost Mitten

**Directions:** Help the girl find her mitten.

## One Step Further
Design a cool pair of mittens to wear in the winter.

# In the Air

**Directions:** Circle the words in the puzzle. The words go across and down.

```
p  f  b  l  i  m  p  y
l  e  g  k  i  t  e  j
a  d  h  i  b  k  z  e
n  x  c  j  m  a  l  t
e  r  o  c  k  e  t  u
w  v  g  l  i  d  e  r
```

 jet

 kite

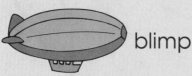 blimp

 plane

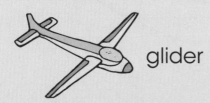 glider

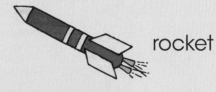 rocket

## One Step Further

Have you ever flown on a plane? Where would you like to fly?

# A Space Trip

**Directions:** Help the rocket get to the moon.

## One Step Further

Imagine you are flying to the moon. What might you see out the window?

# Answer Key

**ANSWER KEY**

### 6 — Same

**Directions:** Color the shape in each row that looks the same as the first shape.

**One Step Further**
Find two objects in your home that are the same shape. What shape are those objects?

Kindergarten Essentials

### 7 — Different

**Directions:** Draw an **X** on the shapes in each row that are different from the first shape.

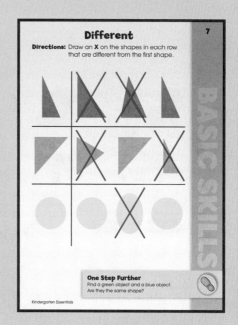

**One Step Further**
Find a green object and a blue object. Are they the same shape?

Kindergarten Essentials

### 8 — Holiday Match

**Directions:** Color the first picture. Color each picture that is the **same** as the first one.

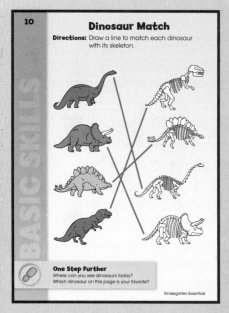

**One Step Further**
Make a holiday card for a friend. Use some of the pictures you see on this page.

Kindergarten Essentials

### 9 — A Complete Picture

**Directions:** Draw the missing parts to make the pictures look the same. Color the pictures with the same colors.

Drawings will vary.

**One Step Further**
Draw a picture. Ask a friend to draw a picture that looks the same as yours.

Kindergarten Essentials

### 10 — Dinosaur Match

**Directions:** Draw a line to match each dinosaur with its skeleton.

**One Step Further**
Where can you see dinosaurs today? Which dinosaur on this page is your favorite?

Kindergarten Essentials

### 11 — Shadow Shapes

**Directions:** Look at the shadow shapes in the first row. Draw a line from each shadow to the picture it matches.

**One Step Further**
Draw what your shadow might look like if you are standing on one leg.

Kindergarten Essentials

Kindergarten Essentials

**BASIC SKILLS**

12

## Same and Different

**Directions:** Color the two pictures in each row that are the same.

**One Step Further**
Find two shirts that you own.
Describe what is different about them.

Kindergarten Essentials

**BASIC SKILLS**

13

## Basketball!

Coby loves to play basketball. In fact, he has six pairs of sneakers just for basketball!

**Directions:** Draw a line to connect each pair of matching shoes.

**One Step Further**
Find a pair of shoes in your home that match. Then, find two shoes that don't match.

Kindergarten Essentials

**BASIC SKILLS**

14

## Pete the Peacock

Look at Pete the Peacock.

**Directions:** Only one of the peacocks below is exactly like Pete. Circle it. What is different about each of the other peacocks?

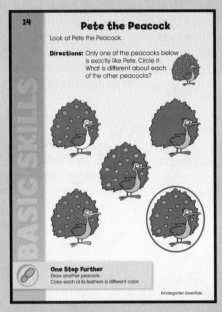

**One Step Further**
Draw another peacock.
Color each of its feathers a different color.

Kindergarten Essentials

**BASIC SKILLS**

15

## Butterfly, Butterflies

A butterfly is a type of insect. It has four wings. Only two of the butterflies below look the same.

**Directions:** Can you find the two matching butterflies? Draw a line to connect them.

**One Step Further**
Can you find two things in your neighborhood that look the same?

Kindergarten Essentials

**BASIC SKILLS**

16

## Opposites

Opposites are things that are different in every way.

**Directions:** Draw a line to match the opposites.

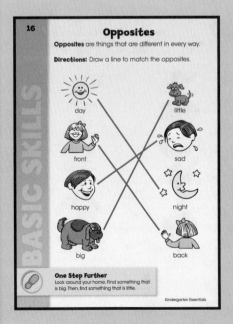

**One Step Further**
Look around your home. Find something that is big. Then, find something that is little.

Kindergarten Essentials

**BASIC SKILLS**

17

## Opposites

**Directions:** Draw a line to match the opposites.

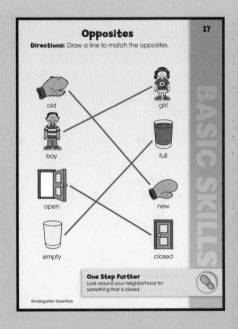

**One Step Further**
Look around your neighborhood for something that is closed.

Kindergarten Essentials

Kindergarten Essentials

**ANSWER KEY**

### 18 — Fast and Slow

**Directions:** Look at the picture below. Circle the things that go fast. Draw an **X** on each thing that goes slow.

**One Step Further**
Sit outside. What can you see that goes fast? What can you see that goes slow?

Kindergarten Essentials

### 19 — Full and Empty

**Directions:** Circle the full container. Draw an **X** on the empty container.

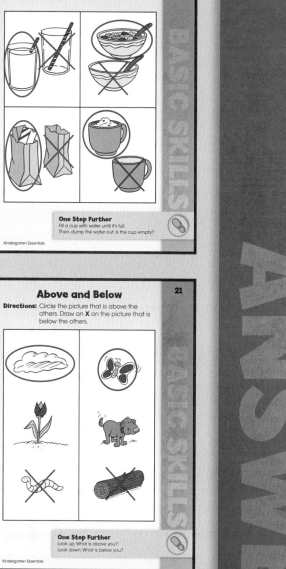

**One Step Further**
Fill a cup with water until it's full. Then, dump the water out. Is the cup empty?

Kindergarten Essentials

### 20 — Taller and Shorter

**Directions:** Circle the picture that is taller. Draw an **X** on the picture that is shorter.

**One Step Further**
Stand next to a friend. Are you taller or shorter?

Kindergarten Essentials

### 21 — Above and Below

**Directions:** Circle the picture that is above the others. Draw an **X** on the picture that is below the others.

**One Step Further**
Look up. What is above you? Look down. What is below you?

Kindergarten Essentials

### 22 — Thanksgiving Day!

Doug just helped his mom set all of the food on the table for Thanksgiving Day. Which things on the table are hot? Which things on the table are cold?

**Directions:** Circle all of the hot things with a red crayon. Circle all of the cold things with a blue crayon.

**One Step Further**
Tell a friend about your favorite Thanksgiving celebration.

Kindergarten Essentials

### 23 — Baseball

Belinda just went to her first baseball game. Many people sat in the bleachers watching it.

**Directions:** Which person is sitting on something soft? Color that person pink. Which person is sitting on something hard? Color that person purple. Which person is happy? Color that person . Which person is sad? Color that person blue. Which person is short? Color that person red. Which person is tall? Color that person orange.

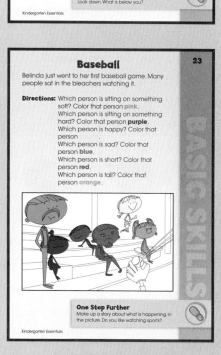

**One Step Further**
Make up a story about what is happening in the picture. Do you like watching sports?

Kindergarten Essentials

Kindergarten Essentials

# 224

## 24 — Things That Go Together

**Directions:** Color the pictures in each row that go together. Draw an **X** on the one that does **not** belong.

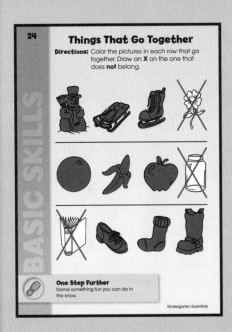

**One Step Further**
Name something fun you can do in the snow.

Kindergarten Essentials

## 25 — Part of a Group

**Directions:** Pick three pictures that go together in each group. Draw an **X** on the picture that does **not** belong in the group.

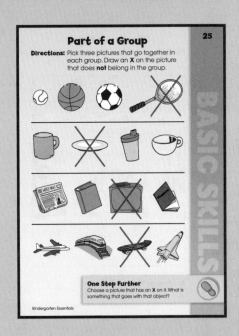

**One Step Further**
Choose a picture that has an **X** on it. What is something that goes with that object?

Kindergarten Essentials

## 26 — You Choose

**Directions:** Look at the animals below.

Which animals have feathers?

Which animals have no legs?

Which animals would be fun to ride?

Answers will vary.

**One Step Further**
Which of the animals on this page would make a good pet? What would you name it?

Kindergarten Essentials

## 27 — The Jungle

Many animals live in the jungle.

**Directions:** Find the animals that are small.

Which animals are large?

Which animals do you think are scaly?

Which animals are soft?

Answers will vary.

**One Step Further**
Name another jungle animal. Describe that animal to a friend.

Kindergarten Essentials

## 28 — So Soft

**Directions:** Which objects below are soft? Color all of the soft things **red**. Color the rest of the objects in a way that makes sense.

Colors will vary.

**One Step Further**
Look around your bedroom for something soft. What did you find?

Kindergarten Essentials

## 29 — Creepy Caves

Many different kinds of animals live in dark caves. Some of the animals pictured below live in caves and some do not. Which animals do not belong?

**Directions:** Draw an **X** on the animals that do **not** belong in a cave.

**One Step Further**
Where do the other animals on this page live?

Kindergarten Essentials

Kindergarten Essentials

30

## What Goes Together?

**Directions:** Draw a line to match each thing that goes together.

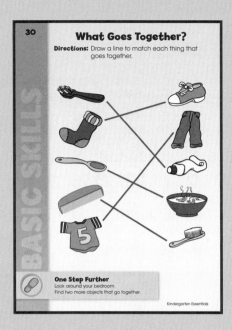

**One Step Further**
Look around your bedroom.
Find two more objects that go together.

Kindergarten Essentials

31

## Three Things

**Directions:** Circle your answers below.

Which three things are on your hand?

Which three things are in the sky?

Which three things would you wear if you were hot?

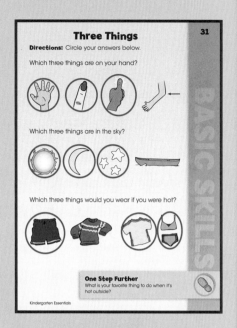

**One Step Further**
What is your favorite thing to do when it's hot outside?

Kindergarten Essentials

32

## Letter Recognition

**Directions:** Circle the letters in each row that match the first letter.

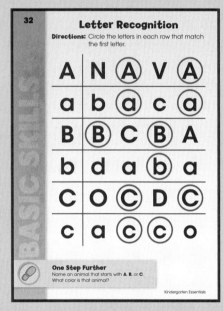

**One Step Further**
Name an animal that starts with **A**, **B**, or **C**.
What color is that animal?

Kindergarten Essentials

33

## Letter Recognition

**Directions:** Circle the letters in each row that match the first letter.

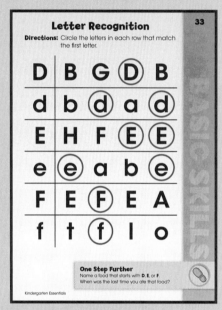

**One Step Further**
Name a food that starts with **D**, **E**, or **F**.
When was the last time you ate that food?

Kindergarten Essentials

34

## Letter Recognition

**Directions:** Circle the letters in each row that match the first letter.

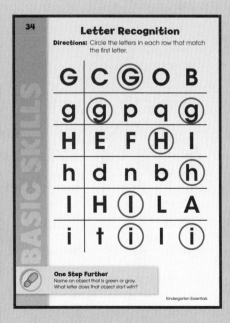

**One Step Further**
Name an object that is green or gray.
What letter does that object start with?

Kindergarten Essentials

35

## Letter Recognition

**Directions:** Circle the letters in each row that match the first letter.

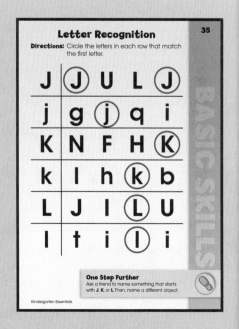

**One Step Further**
Ask a friend to name something that starts
with **J**, **K**, or **L**. Then, name a different object.

Kindergarten Essentials

Kindergarten Essentials

ANSWER KEY

BASIC SKILLS

**36** **Letter Recognition**

**Directions:** Circle the letters in each row that match the first letter.

| M | H | (M) | n | L |
| m | (M) | a | (m) | n |
| N | (M) | (N) | m | (N) |
| n | (n) | m | a | (n) |
| O | (O) | D | B | (O) |
| o | a | (O) | c | (o) |

**One Step Further**
Draw an oval. Draw something that starts with the letter **O** inside the oval.

Kindergarten Essentials

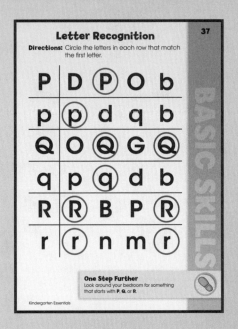

**37** **Letter Recognition**

**Directions:** Circle the letters in each row that match the first letter.

| P | D | (P) | O | b |
| p | (p) | d | q | b |
| Q | O | (Q) | G | (Q) |
| q | p | (q) | d | b |
| R | (R) | B | P | (R) |
| r | (r) | n | m | (r) |

**One Step Further**
Look around your bedroom for something that starts with **P, Q,** or **R.**

Kindergarten Essentials

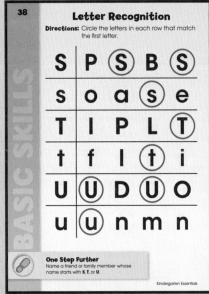

**38** **Letter Recognition**

**Directions:** Circle the letters in each row that match the first letter.

| S | P | (S) | B | (S) |
| s | o | a | (s) | e |
| T | I | P | L | (T) |
| t | f | l | (t) | i |
| U | (U) | D | (U) | O |
| u | (u) | n | m | n |

**One Step Further**
Name a friend or family member whose name starts with **S, T,** or **U.**

Kindergarten Essentials

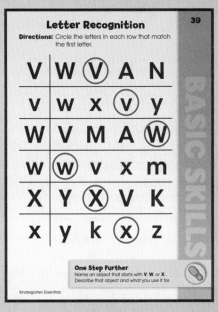

**39** **Letter Recognition**

**Directions:** Circle the letters in each row that match the first letter.

| V | W | (V) | A | N |
| v | w | x | (v) | y |
| W | V | M | A | (W) |
| w | (w) | v | x | m |
| X | Y | (X) | V | K |
| x | y | k | (x) | z |

**One Step Further**
Name an object that starts with **V, W,** or **X.** Describe that object and what you use it for.

Kindergarten Essentials

**40** **Letter Recognition**

**Directions:** Circle the letters in each row that match the first letter.

| Y | W | (Y) | V | X |
| y | w | x | v | (y) |
| Z | N | M | (Z) | W |
| z | n | (z) | x | m |

**One Step Further**
Draw a picture of a zebra you might see during a day at the zoo.

Kindergarten Essentials

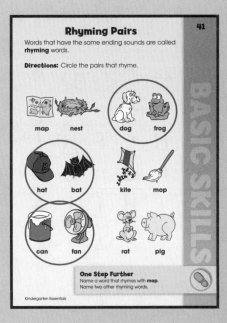

**41** **Rhyming Pairs**

Words that have the same ending sounds are called **rhyming** words.

**Directions:** Circle the pairs that rhyme.

map    nest    dog    frog

hat    bat    kite    mop

can    fan    rat    pig

**One Step Further**
Name a word that rhymes with **map.** Name two other rhyming words.

Kindergarten Essentials

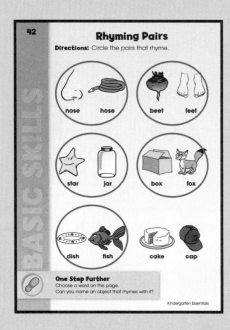

**42 Rhyming Pairs**

**Directions:** Circle the pairs that rhyme.

nose — hose • beet — feet • star — jar • box — fox • dish — fish • cake — cap

**One Step Further**
Choose a word on this page.
Can you name an object that rhymes with it?

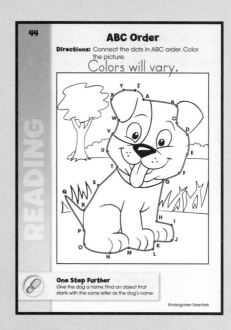

**44 ABC Order**

**Directions:** Connect the dots in ABC order. Color the picture.

Colors will vary.

**One Step Further**
Give the dog a name. Find an object that starts with the same letter as the dog's name.

**45 Buddy's Basket**

Buddy is putting things in his basket. He wants only things that begin with **Bb**.

**Directions:** Color the pictures of things that begin with **Bb**.

**One Step Further**
Look around your room for objects to add to Buddy's basket.

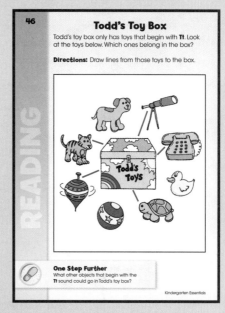

**46 Todd's Toy Box**

Todd's toy box only has toys that begin with **Tt**. Look at the toys below. Which ones belong in the box?

**Directions:** Draw lines from those toys to the box.

**One Step Further**
What other objects that begin with the **Tt** sound could go in Todd's toy box?

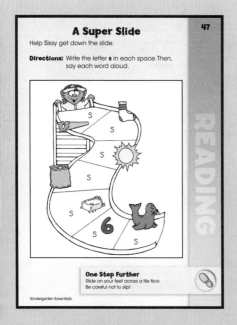

**47 A Super Slide**

Help Sissy get down the slide.

**Directions:** Write the letter **s** in each space. Then, say each word aloud.

**One Step Further**
Slide on your feet across a tile floor. Be careful not to slip!

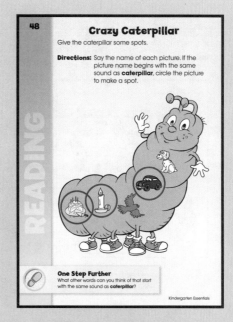

**48 Crazy Caterpillar**

Give the caterpillar some spots.

**Directions:** Say the name of each picture. If the picture name begins with the same sound as **caterpillar**, circle the picture to make a spot.

**One Step Further**
What other words can you think of that start with the same sound as **caterpillar**?

ANSWER KEY

**228**

ANSWER KEY

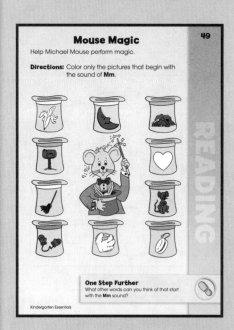

### Mouse Magic
Help Michael Mouse perform magic.

**Directions:** Color only the pictures that begin with the sound of **Mm**.

**One Step Further**
What other words can you think of that start with the **Mm** sound?

Kindergarten Essentials

49

READING

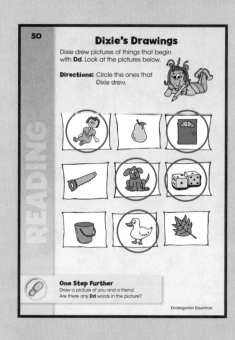

50

### Dixie's Drawings
Dixie drew pictures of things that begin with **Dd**. Look at the pictures below.

**Directions:** Circle the ones that Dixie drew.

**One Step Further**
Draw a picture of you and a friend. Are there any **Dd** words in the picture?

Kindergarten Essentials

READING

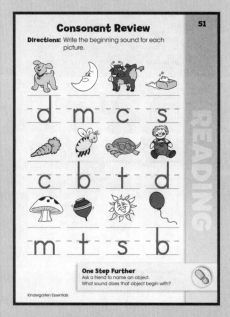

### Consonant Review
**Directions:** Write the beginning sound for each picture.

d m c s

c b t d

m t s b

**One Step Further**
Ask a friend to name an object. What sound does that object begin with?

Kindergarten Essentials

51

READING

52

### Wonderful Wagon
The wagon can carry only pictures whose names begin with the sound of **Ww**.

**Directions:** Color the pictures that can go in the wagon.

**One Step Further**
Look at a wall in the room you are in. What is on the wall?

Kindergarten Essentials

READING

### Jump, Jake, Jump!
Help Jake jump along the path.

**Directions:** Write the letter **j** on the lines to complete the words. Then, say each word aloud.

j am    j et
j ar
j acks
j ug
j eep    j eans

**One Step Further**
Name a friend whose name starts with the letter **J**.

Kindergarten Essentials

53

READING

54

### Fishing Fun
These monsters are fishing for things that begin with **Ff**.

**Directions:** Draw a line from each hook to a fish that has something beginning with **Ff**.

**One Step Further**
What is your favorite food? Draw food for the fish to eat.

Kindergarten Essentials

READING

Kindergarten Essentials

### Rain, Rain, Go Away
**55**

**Directions:** Color the raindrops that have pictures that begin with **Rr**.

**One Step Further**
What is your favorite thing to do when it's raining?

Kindergarten Essentials

---

**56**
### Pizza Party

Look at the picture.

**Directions:** Circle eight things that begin with **Pp**.

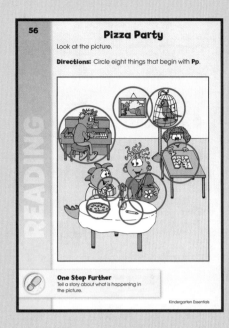

**One Step Further**
Tell a story about what is happening in the picture.

Kindergarten Essentials

---

### In Huey's House
**57**

Find the seven **Hh** things in Huey's house.

**Directions:** Color them **red**. Then, color the rest of the picture.

Colors will vary.

**One Step Further**
Find seven red things in your home. Do any of them begin with the **Hh** sound?

Kindergarten Essentials

---

**58**
### Handy Norman

Norman loves the letter **Nn**!

**Directions:** Draw a line from each of Norman's hands to a picture of something that begins with **Nn**.

**One Step Further**
Grab a net and go outside. What can you catch in the net?

Kindergarten Essentials

---

### Special Keys
**59**

Each monster has a key. The keys will open only chests that have pictures of things beginning with **Kk**.

**Directions:** Circle the chests the keys will open.

**One Step Further**
Ask an adult to give you a key. Try to find out what it unlocks.

Kindergarten Essentials

---

**60**
### Very Vivid Vs

**Directions:** Draw a line from **Vv** to each picture that begins with the sound of **Vv**. Then, color the **Vv** pictures.

Vv

**One Step Further**
Make a valentine for a friend. Decorate it using your favorite shapes and colors.

Kindergarten Essentials

---

READING

ANSWER KEY

Kindergarten Essentials

ANSWER KEY

**Light It Up!**                                    61

**Directions:** Draw a line from the light to each picture that begins with the sound of **Ll**. Then, color the **Ll** pictures.

**One Step Further**
Find an object in your home that starts with the **Ll** sound.

Kindergarten Essentials

62    **A Great Garden of Gs**

**Directions:** Write **g** under each picture that begins with the sound of **g**. Color the **g** pictures.

**One Step Further**
Look outside. What do you see that starts with the **Gg** sound?

Kindergarten Essentials

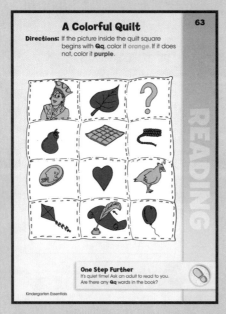

**A Colorful Quilt**                                63

**Directions:** If the picture inside the quilt square begins with **Qq**, color it **orange**. If it does not, color it **purple**.

**One Step Further**
It's quiet time! Ask an adult to read to you. Are there any **Qq** words in the book?

Kindergarten Essentials

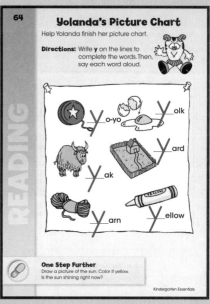

64    **Yolanda's Picture Chart**

Help Yolanda finish her picture chart.

**Directions:** Write **y** on the lines to complete the words. Then, say each word aloud.

**One Step Further**
Draw a picture of the sun. Color it yellow. Is the sun shining right now?

Kindergarten Essentials

**Zep Zebra's Zoo**                                 65

Zep Zebra likes living in the zoo.

**Directions:** Color each picture that begins with the sound of **Zz**.

**One Step Further**
Tell a story about a day at the zoo. What is your favorite zoo animal?

Kindergarten Essentials

66    **Consonant Review**

Say the name of each picture.

**Directions:** Write the letter that makes the beginning sound.

**One Step Further**
What letter does your name start with? Is that letter a consonant?

Kindergarten Essentials

Kindergarten Essentials

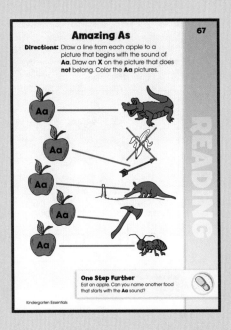

### Amazing As
**67**

**Directions:** Draw a line from each apple to a picture that begins with the sound of **Aa**. Draw an **X** on the picture that does **not** belong. Color the **Aa** pictures.

**One Step Further**
Eat an apple. Can you name another food that starts with the **Aa** sound?

Kindergarten Essentials

**68**
### Andy's Pictures

Help Andy label his pictures below and on page 69.

**Directions:** Trace the words. Then, say the words aloud. Listen to the sound that **Aa** makes.

ant

ax

**One Step Further**
Draw something else that Andy might have a picture of.

Kindergarten Essentials

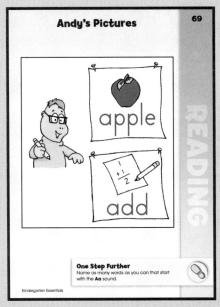

### Andy's Pictures
**69**

apple

add

**One Step Further**
Name as many words as you can that start with the **Aa** sound.

Kindergarten Essentials

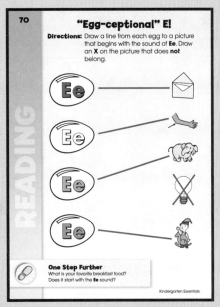

**70**
### "Egg-ceptional" E!

**Directions:** Draw a line from each egg to a picture that begins with the sound of **Ee**. Draw an **X** on the picture that does **not** belong.

**One Step Further**
What is your favorite breakfast food? Does it start with the **Ee** sound?

Kindergarten Essentials

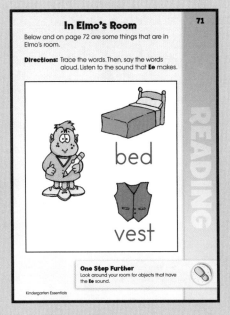

### In Elmo's Room
**71**

Below and on page 72 are some things that are in Elmo's room.

**Directions:** Trace the words. Then, say the words aloud. Listen to the sound that **Ee** makes.

bed

vest

**One Step Further**
Look around your room for objects that have the **Ee** sound.

Kindergarten Essentials

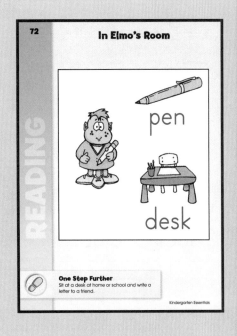

**72**
### In Elmo's Room

pen

desk

**One Step Further**
Sit at a desk at home or school and write a letter to a friend.

Kindergarten Essentials

ANSWER KEY

### Make a Wish
73

The monsters are at a wishing well. Find out what each one is hoping to get.

**Directions:** Write **i** on the lines to complete each word. Then, say the words aloud.

**One Step Further**
Pretend you are at a wishing well. What would you wish for?

Kindergarten Essentials

### Izzy's Gifts
74

Look at Izzy's birthday gifts! Help her label them.

**Directions:** Trace the words below and on page 75. Then, say the words aloud. Listen to the sound that **Ii** makes.

dish    mitt

**One Step Further**
Grab a mitt and play catch with a friend. How many times did you catch the ball?

Kindergarten Essentials

### Izzy's Gifts
75

pig    fish

**One Step Further**
What gifts do you want to give a friend for his or her next birthday?

Kindergarten Essentials

### Oo Animal Search
76

Can you find the **Oo** animals?

**Directions:** Trace each **Oo**. Color the animals that begin with the sound of **Oo**.

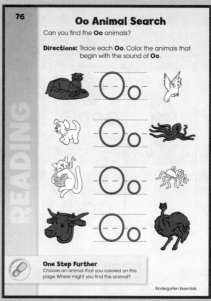

**One Step Further**
Choose an animal that you colored on this page. Where might you find this animal?

Kindergarten Essentials

### Olive's Box
77

What things are in Olive's box?

**Directions:** Trace the words below and on page 78. Then, say the words aloud. Listen to the sound that **Oo** makes.

sock    clock

**One Step Further**
Look around your home for a sock and a clock. Where did you find these objects?

Kindergarten Essentials

### Olive's Box
78

top    doll

**One Step Further**
Work with a friend to name as many words with the **Oo** sound as you can.

Kindergarten Essentials

Kindergarten Essentials

# Unusual Umbrellas
79

**Directions:** Draw a line from each child to a picture that begins with the sound of **Uu**.

**One Step Further**
Pretend it's raining and stand under an umbrella.

Kindergarten Essentials

---

80
# Ug's Puppets

Ug collects puppets. Some of his puppets are shown below and on page 81.

**Directions:** Trace the words. Then, say the words aloud. Listen to the sound that **Uu** makes.

bug    cub

**One Step Further**
Ask an adult to help make a puppet of your own. Put on a puppet show!

Kindergarten Essentials

---

# Ug's Puppets
81

duck    pup

**One Step Further**
Tell a story about a pup and a duck. Make puppets if you want!

Kindergarten Essentials

---

82
# Animal Snapshots

**Directions:** Write **a, e, i, o,** or **u** on each line.

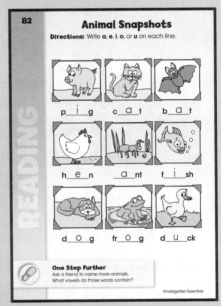

p_i_g    c_a_t    b_a_t

h_e_n    _a_nt    f_i_sh

d_o_g    fr_o_g    d_u_ck

**One Step Further**
Ask a friend to name more animals. What vowels do those words contain?

Kindergarten Essentials

---

# Strawberry Patch Match
83

**Directions:** Draw a line from each uppercase letter to its lowercase letter.

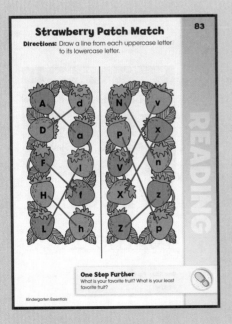

**One Step Further**
What is your favorite fruit? What is your least favorite fruit?

Kindergarten Essentials

---

84
# See the Shells

**Directions:** Draw a line from each uppercase letter to its lowercase letter.

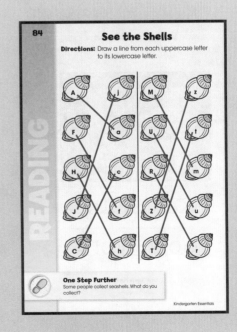

**One Step Further**
Some people collect seashells. What do you collect?

Kindergarten Essentials

---

ANSWER KEY

# 234

ANSWER KEY

## Haystack Match
85

**Directions:** Draw a line from each uppercase letter to its lowercase letter.

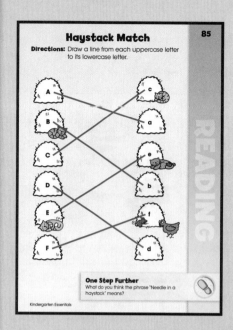

**One Step Further**
What do you think the phrase "Needle in a haystack" means?

Kindergarten Essentials

## Make a Match
86

**Directions:** Draw a line from each uppercase letter to its lowercase letter.

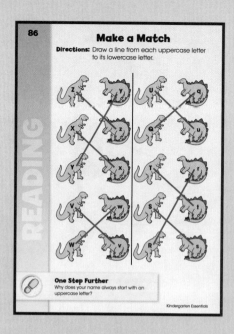

**One Step Further**
Why does your name always start with an uppercase letter?

Kindergarten Essentials

## A Long Time Ago
87

**Directions:** Color the picture. Then, trace the words below.

dinosaurs

trees grass

**One Step Further**
Have you ever seen a real dinosaur? Why or why not?

Kindergarten Essentials

## Tractor Pull
88

**Directions:** Color the picture of the farm. Then, trace the words below.

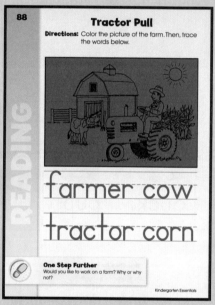

farmer cow

tractor corn

**One Step Further**
Would you like to work on a farm? Why or why not?

Kindergarten Essentials

## Building a House
89

**Directions:** Color the picture. Then, trace the words below.

wood house

tools work

**One Step Further**
Tell a story about a time that you worked hard for something.

Kindergarten Essentials

## You've Arrived!
90

**Directions:** Color the picture. Then, trace the words below.

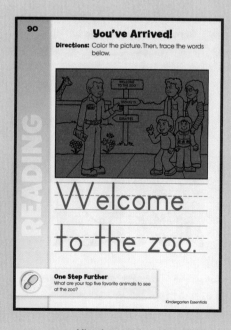

Welcome

to the zoo.

**One Step Further**
What are your top five favorite animals to see at the zoo?

Kindergarten Essentials

READING

Kindergarten Essentials

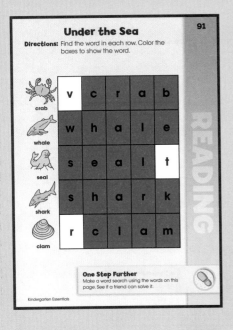

### Under the Sea
**91**

**Directions:** Find the word in each row. Color the boxes to show the word.

| crab | v | c | r | a | b |
| whale | w | h | a | l | e |
| seal | s | e | a | l | t |
| shark | s | h | a | r | k |
| clam | r | c | l | a | m |

**One Step Further**
Make a word search using the words on this page. See if a friend can solve it.

Kindergarten Essentials

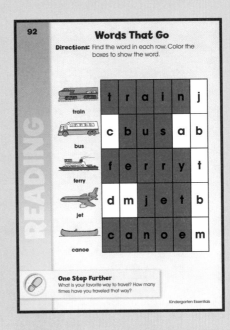

### Words That Go
**92**

**Directions:** Find the word in each row. Color the boxes to show the word.

| train | t | r | a | i | n | j |
| bus | c | b | u | s | a | b |
| ferry | f | e | r | r | y | t |
| jet | d | m | j | e | t | b |
| canoe | c | a | n | o | e | m |

**One Step Further**
What is your favorite way to travel? How many times have you traveled that way?

Kindergarten Essentials

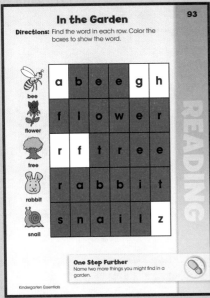

### In the Garden
**93**

**Directions:** Find the word in each row. Color the boxes to show the word.

| bee | a | b | e | e | g | h |
| flower | f | l | o | w | e | r |
| tree | r | f | t | r | e | e |
| rabbit | r | a | b | b | i | t |
| snail | s | n | a | i | l | z |

**One Step Further**
Name two more things you might find in a garden.

Kindergarten Essentials

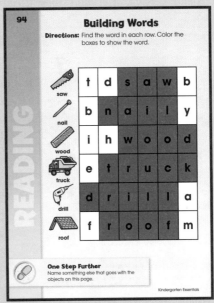

### Building Words
**94**

**Directions:** Find the word in each row. Color the boxes to show the word.

| saw | t | d | s | a | w | b |
| nail | b | n | a | i | l | y |
| wood | i | h | w | o | o | d |
| truck | e | t | r | u | c | k |
| drill | d | r | i | l | l | a |
| roof | f | r | o | o | f | m |

**One Step Further**
Name something else that goes with the objects on this page.

Kindergarten Essentials

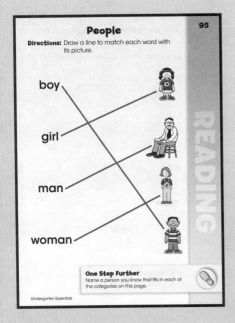

### People
**95**

**Directions:** Draw a line to match each word with its picture.

boy

girl

man

woman

**One Step Further**
Name a person you know that fits in each of the categories on this page.

Kindergarten Essentials

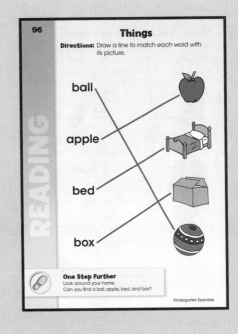

### Things
**96**

**Directions:** Draw a line to match each word with its picture.

ball

apple

bed

box

**One Step Further**
Look around your home. Can you find a ball, apple, bed, and box?

Kindergarten Essentials

**Kindergarten Essentials**

ANSWER KEY
READING

ANSWER KEY

### Action Words

**Directions:** Draw a line to match the action word with the person doing that action.

97

walk
run
talk
eat

**One Step Further**
Show how you can do each of the action words on this page.

Kindergarten Essentials

98

### Action Words

**Directions:** Draw a line to match the action word with the person doing that action.

play
ride
sit
cook

**One Step Further**
What is your favorite thing to do after school—play, ride, sit, or cook?

Kindergarten Essentials

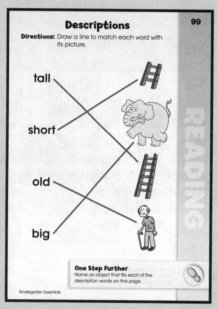

### Descriptions

99

**Directions:** Draw a line to match each word with its picture.

tall
short
old
big

**One Step Further**
Name an object that fits each of the description words on this page.

Kindergarten Essentials

100

### Descriptions

**Directions:** Draw a line to match each word with its picture.

little
happy
sad
funny

**One Step Further**
Name something that makes you happy. Name something you think is funny.

Kindergarten Essentials

### Which Items Do You Not Need?

101

Lauren and her dad want to play tennis.

**Directions:** Draw an **X** on the things they do **not** need to play tennis.

**One Step Further**
What things do you need to play your favorite sport?

Kindergarten Essentials

102

### Which Items Do You Not Need?

Lloyd is working at a bakery.

**Directions:** Draw an **X** on the things he will **not** need to do his job well.

**One Step Further**
What might Lloyd be baking today? Do you like to bake?

Kindergarten Essentials

Kindergarten Essentials

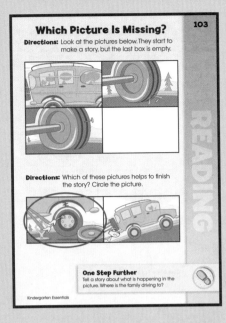

### Which Picture Is Missing? 103

**Directions:** Look at the pictures below. They start to make a story, but the last box is empty.

**Directions:** Which of these pictures helps to finish the story? Circle the picture.

**One Step Further**
Tell a story about what is happening in the picture. Where is the family driving to?

Kindergarten Essentials

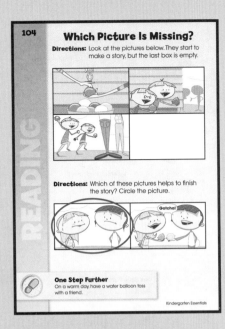

### 104 Which Picture Is Missing?

**Directions:** Look at the pictures below. They start to make a story, but the last box is empty.

**Directions:** Which of these pictures helps to finish the story? Circle the picture.

**One Step Further**
On a warm day, have a water balloon toss with a friend.

Kindergarten Essentials

### Rainbow Clues 105

**Directions:** Follow the clues below. Circle your choices.

Find the object that is **brown** and **hard**.

Find the object that is _____ and **long**.

Find the object that is **blue** and **tiny**.

**One Step Further**
Choose an object on this page. Give a friend two clues that describe the object.

Kindergarten Essentials

### 106 Color It Again

**Directions:** Color the picture in each row that both words describe.

**round** and _orange_

**scared** and **brown**

**wet** and **pointy**

**One Step Further**
Find an object in your school that is big and brown. What did you find?

Kindergarten Essentials

### Grandma Gertie 107

Grandma Gertie loves flowers.

**Directions:** Use the clues below to find the perfect flower for Grandma. Circle your answer.

Grandma likes flowers that are _pink_.
She likes flowers that are tall.
She likes flowers that come with candy.

**One Step Further**
What do you think makes the perfect flower? Draw it and give it to a friend.

Kindergarten Essentials

### 108 Jalen's Vacation

Jalen wants to go on vacation. Help him pick out the best spot for his trip.

**Directions:** Read the clues below. Circle the trip that Jalen should pick.

Jalen does not want to go to a cold place.
Jalen does not want to go to a beach.
Jalen wants to go to a place with games.

**One Step Further**
Where would you most like to go on vacation? What would you do there?

Kindergarten Essentials

ANSWER KEY

**238**

ANSWER KEY

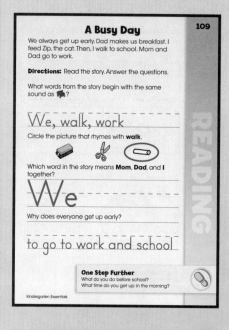

### A Busy Day

**109**

We always get up early. Dad makes us breakfast. I feed Zip, the cat. Then, I walk to school. Mom and Dad go to work.

**Directions:** Read the story. Answer the questions.

What words from the story begin with the same sound as 🚢?

We, walk, work

Circle the picture that rhymes with **walk**.

Which word in the story means **Mom**, **Dad**, and **I** together?

We

Why does everyone get up early?

to go to work and school

READING

**One Step Further**
What do you do before school?
What time do you get up in the morning?

Kindergarten Essentials

**110**

### The Goat

On Saturday, Grandma and I went bike riding. Grandma wore her straw hat. We rode along the bike path to the high school. We went to the farm animal show. We got to pet the goats. Grandma left her hat on the bike seat. A goat ate the hat!

**Directions:** Read the story. Answer the questions.

Circle the picture that has the sound of **e** in **pet**.

Circle the picture that names a word that rhymes with **goat**.

Which word in the story is a day of the week?

Saturday

Where does the bike path go?

high school

READING

**One Step Further**
Where is your favorite place to ride your bike?
Is there a bike path near your home?

Kindergarten Essentials

### Antarctic Penguins

**111**

Penguins are birds but they don't fly. Penguins swim. Penguins lay eggs. Most penguin chicks have fluffy feathers. Penguins live in large groups.

**Directions:** Read the story. Answer the questions.

Circle the picture whose name begins with the blend you hear at the beginning of **fluffy**.

What word from the story rhymes with **legs**?

eggs

What word from the story means the same as **do not**?

don't

Do all birds fly?

no

READING

**One Step Further**
Where do penguins live?
Have you ever seen a penguin?

Kindergarten Essentials

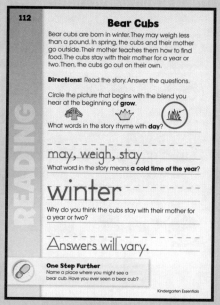

**112**

### Bear Cubs

Bear cubs are born in winter. They may weigh less than a pound. In spring, the cubs and their mother go outside. Their mother teaches them how to find food. The cubs stay with their mother for a year or two. Then, the cubs go out on their own.

**Directions:** Read the story. Answer the questions.

Circle the picture that begins with the blend you hear at the beginning of **grow**.

What words in the story rhyme with **day**?

may, weigh, stay

What word in the story means **a cold time of the year**?

winter

Why do you think the cubs stay with their mother for a year or two?

Answers will vary.

READING

**One Step Further**
Name a place where you might see a
bear cub. Have you ever seen a bear cub?

Kindergarten Essentials

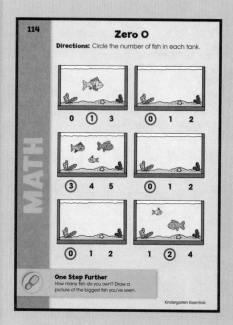

**114**

### Zero 0

**Directions:** Circle the number of fish in each tank.

MATH

**One Step Further**
How many fish do you own? Draw a
picture of the biggest fish you've seen.

Kindergarten Essentials

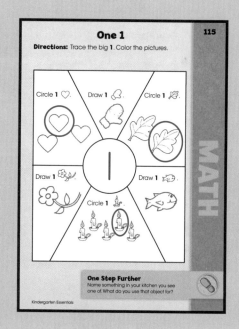

### One 1

**115**

**Directions:** Trace the big **1**. Color the pictures.

MATH

**One Step Further**
Name something in your kitchen you see
one of. What do you use that object for?

Kindergarten Essentials

Kindergarten Essentials

## 116 — Two 2

**Directions:** Help the bunny twins catch their balloons. Follow the twos through the maze.

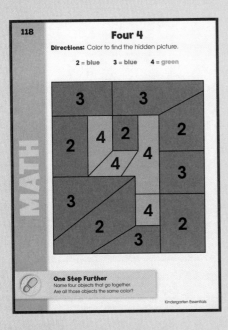

**One Step Further**
Look around your neighborhood. Name something you see two of.

Kindergarten Essentials

## 117 — Three 3

**Directions:** Count and write the number in each box. Circle the groups of three. Color the groups of four.

4    3
4    3

**One Step Further**
Name three more fruits. Which is your favorite?

Kindergarten Essentials

## 118 — Four 4

**Directions:** Color to find the hidden picture.

2 = blue    3 = blue    4 = green

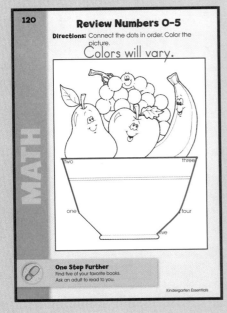

**One Step Further**
Name four objects that go together. Are all those objects the same color?

Kindergarten Essentials

## 119 — Five 5

**Directions:** Five dogs are colored. Color five dogs.

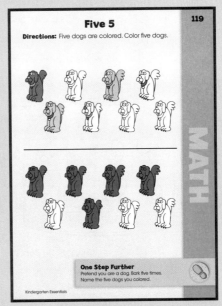

**One Step Further**
Pretend you are a dog. Bark five times. Name the five dogs you colored.

Kindergarten Essentials

## 120 — Review Numbers 0–5

**Directions:** Connect the dots in order. Color the picture.

Colors will vary.

**One Step Further**
Find five of your favorite books. Ask an adult to read to you.

Kindergarten Essentials

## 121 — Six 6

**Directions:** Count and color each picture. Circle each group of six.

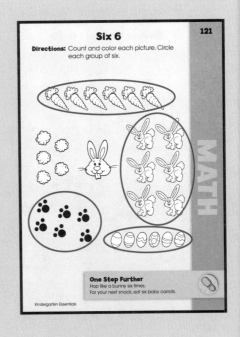

**One Step Further**
Hop like a bunny six times. For your next snack, eat six baby carrots.

Kindergarten Essentials

Kindergarten Essentials

ANSWER KEY

**122**    **Seven 7**

**Directions:** Draw seven cookies.

**One Step Further**
Some people think seven is a lucky number.
What is your lucky number?

Kindergarten Essentials

---

**123**    **Eight 8**

**Directions:** Count and color eight pieces of gold in each of the treasure chests. Then, color the treasure chests.

Colors will vary.

**One Step Further**
Name other things you might find in a treasure chest.

Kindergarten Essentials

---

**124**    **Nine 9**

**Directions:** Draw nine ◯'s in the ⬜. Color the ◯'s.

Colors will vary.

**One Step Further**
Put a handful of jellybeans in a jar.
Ask a friend to guess how many are in the jar.

Kindergarten Essentials

---

**125**    **Ten 10**

**Directions:** Color five dots **red**, three dots **blue**, and two dots **orange** on the butterfly. Count the dots on the butterfly.

How many are there altogether? ___10___

**One Step Further**
Draw a picture of the prettiest butterfly you've seen.

Kindergarten Essentials

---

**126**    **Review Numbers 0–10**

**Directions:** Count the beads in each row. Write the number.

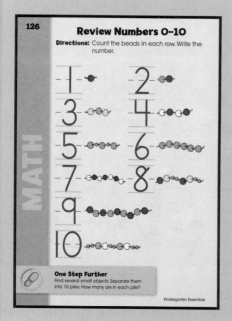

**One Step Further**
Find several small objects. Separate them into 10 piles. How many are in each pile?

Kindergarten Essentials

---

**127**    **Numbers 1–10**

**Directions:** Circle the words in the puzzle. The words go across and down.

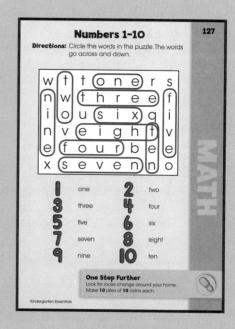

1   one    2   two
3   three    4   four
5   five    6   six
7   seven    8   eight
9   nine    10   ten

**One Step Further**
Look for loose change around your home.
Make **10** piles of **10** coins each.

Kindergarten Essentials

**Kindergarten Essentials**

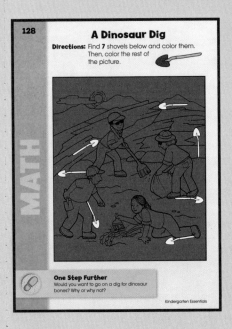

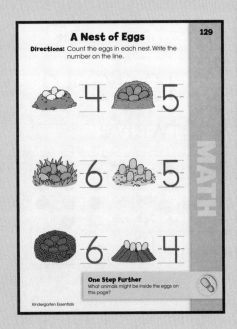

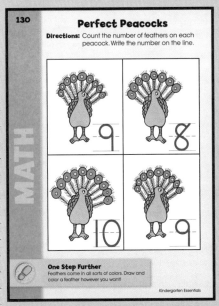

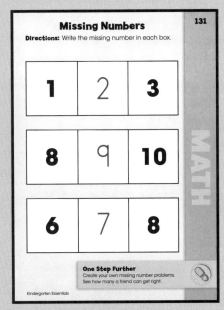

**ANSWER KEY**

ANSWER KEY

MATH

**134**
### Trace and Write 12
**Directions:** Trace and write the number **12**. Then, count and write the numbers.

12 12 12

twelve

12

11

**One Step Further**
How many balls can you find in your school? What do you like to do on the playground?

Kindergarten Essentials

**135**
### Twelve 12
**Directions:** Count each group of creatures. Draw a line from the creatures to their matching apples.

**One Step Further**
Sit outside for awhile. How many birds do you see? How many butterflies do you see?

Kindergarten Essentials

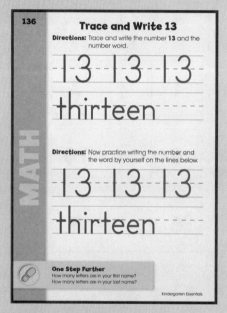

**136**
### Trace and Write 13
**Directions:** Trace and write the number **13** and the number word.

13 13 13

thirteen

**Directions:** Now practice writing the number and the word by yourself on the lines below.

13 13 13

thirteen

**One Step Further**
How many letters are in your first name? How many letters are in your last name?

Kindergarten Essentials

**137**
### Thirteen 13
**Directions:** Color the number. Color the word. Count and color the rest of the picture.

13 thirteen

**One Step Further**
Look at the front lawn of your home or school. Name 13 things you see.

Kindergarten Essentials

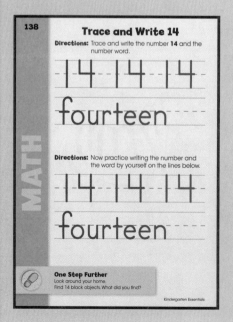

**138**
### Trace and Write 14
**Directions:** Trace and write the number **14** and the number word.

14 14 14

fourteen

**Directions:** Now practice writing the number and the word by yourself on the lines below.

14 14 14

fourteen

**One Step Further**
Look around your home. Find 14 black objects. What did you find?

Kindergarten Essentials

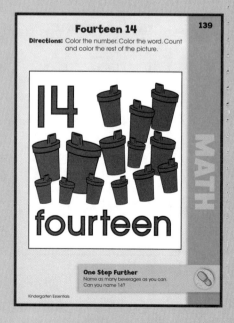

**139**
### Fourteen 14
**Directions:** Color the number. Color the word. Count and color the rest of the picture.

14 fourteen

**One Step Further**
Name as many beverages as you can. Can you name 14?

Kindergarten Essentials

Kindergarten Essentials

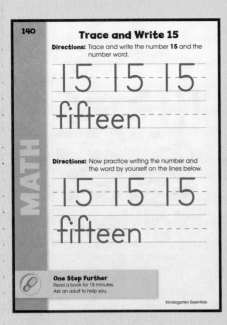

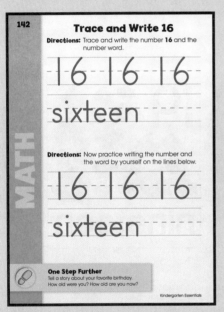

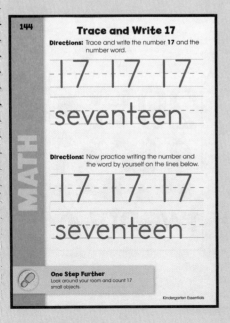

ANSWER KEY

**244**

MATH

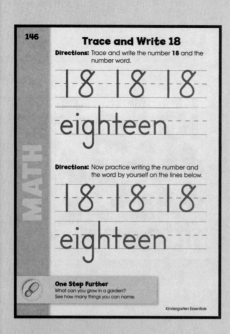

146
**Trace and Write 18**
**Directions:** Trace and write the number **18** and the number word.

18  18  18

eighteen

**Directions:** Now practice writing the number and the word by yourself on the lines below.

18  18  18

eighteen

**One Step Further**
What can you grow in a garden?
See how many things you can name.

Kindergarten Essentials

147
**Eighteen 18**
**Directions:** Color the number. Color the word. Count and color the rest of the picture.

18
eighteen

**One Step Further**
Describe a worm to a friend.
Tell a story about the worm.

MATH

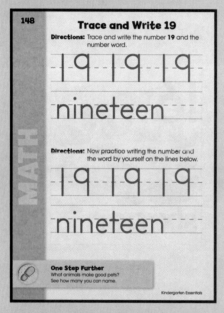

148
**Trace and Write 19**
**Directions:** Trace and write the number **19** and the number word.

19  19  19

nineteen

**Directions:** Now practice writing the number and the word by yourself on the lines below.

19  19  19

nineteen

**One Step Further**
What animals make good pets?
See how many you can name.

Kindergarten Essentials

149
**Nineteen 19**
**Directions:** Color the number. Color the word. Count and color the rest of the picture.

19
nineteen

**One Step Further**
Name the fish in this picture.
Where do you think the fish are swimming?

Kindergarten Essentials

MATH

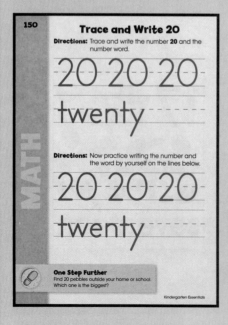

150
**Trace and Write 20**
**Directions:** Trace and write the number **20** and the number word.

20 20 20

twenty

**Directions:** Now practice writing the number and the word by yourself on the lines below.

20 20 20

twenty

**One Step Further**
Find 20 pebbles outside your home or school.
Which one is the biggest?

Kindergarten Essentials

151
**Twenty 20**
**Directions:** Color the number. Color the word. Count and color the rest of the picture.

20
twenty

**One Step Further**
Find 20 of your favorite objects.
Put them in order from biggest to smallest.

Kindergarten Essentials

MATH

Kindergarten Essentials

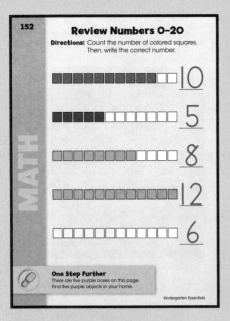

### Review Numbers 0–20

**Directions:** Count the number of colored squares. Then, write the correct number.

10

5

8

12

6

**One Step Further**
There are five purple boxes on this page. Find five purple objects in your home.

*Kindergarten Essentials*

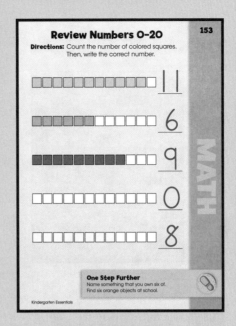

### Review Numbers 0–20

**Directions:** Count the number of colored squares. Then, write the correct number.

11

6

9

0

8

**One Step Further**
Name something that you own six of. Find six orange objects at school.

*Kindergarten Essentials*

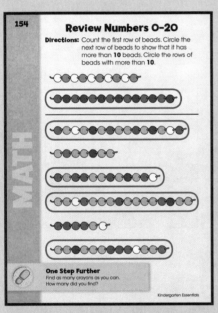

### Review Numbers 0–20

**Directions:** Count the first row of beads. Circle the next row of beads to show that it has more than **10** beads. Circle the rows of beads with more than **10**.

**One Step Further**
Find as many crayons as you can. How many did you find?

*Kindergarten Essentials*

### Review Numbers 0–20

**Directions:** Connect the dots in order from **1** to **20**. Color the surprise!

Colors will vary.

**One Step Further**
Look out the window. Count the cars you see until you get to 20.

*Kindergarten Essentials*

### Happy Hippo

**Directions:** Write the missing numbers. Color the picture.

Colors will vary.

| 1 | 2 | 3 | 4 | 5 |
|---|---|---|---|---|
| 6 | 7 | 8 | 9 | 10 |
| 11 | 12 | 13 | 14 | 15 |
| 16 | 17 | 18 | 19 | 20 |

**One Step Further**
Count to **20** as fast as you can. Ask an adult to time you.

*Kindergarten Essentials*

### Spotty Leopards

**Directions:** Circle the number of spots on each leopard.

17  (18)  19

17  18  (19)

17  18  (19)

(17)  18  19

**One Step Further**
Draw another animal that has spots. Draw **19** spots on the animal.

*Kindergarten Essentials*

ANSWER KEY

**246**

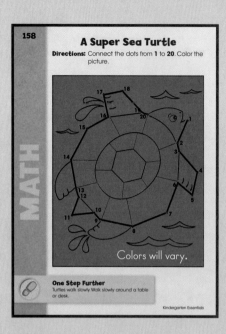

**158 — A Super Sea Turtle**
Directions: Connect the dots from 1 to 20. Color the picture.
Colors will vary.

One Step Further
Turtles walk slowly. Walk slowly around a table or desk.

**159 — Time to Sleep**
Directions: Connect the dots from 1 to 20. Color the picture.
Colors will vary.

One Step Further
What is your favorite activity to do with an adult?

**160 — Elephant Snacks**
Directions: Count the peanuts in each bag. Then, write the number on the line.
15  14  16

One Step Further
Count the peanuts on this page. How many peanuts can each elephant eat?

**161 — Feeding the Birds**
Directions: Draw 15 more pieces of birdseed in the bag. Then, answer the question below.

How many pieces of birdseed are in the bag now? 20

One Step Further
With an adult, make a bird feeder. Fill it with birdseed and put it outside your home.

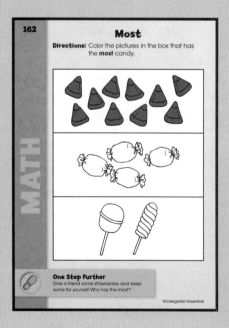

**162 — Most**
Directions: Color the pictures in the box that has the **most** candy.

One Step Further
Give a friend some strawberries and keep some for yourself. Who has the most?

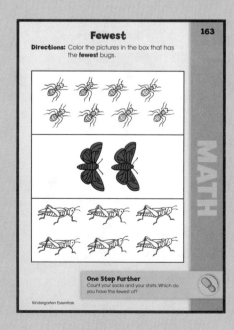

**163 — Fewest**
Directions: Color the pictures in the box that has the **fewest** bugs.

One Step Further
Count your socks and your shirts. Which do you have the fewest of?

Kindergarten Essentials

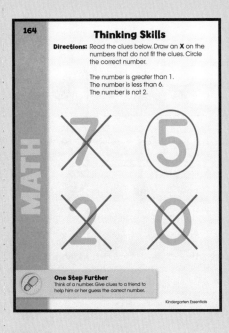

### 164 Thinking Skills

**Directions:** Read the clues below. Draw an **X** on the numbers that do not fit the clues. Circle the correct number.

The number is greater than 1.
The number is less than 6.
The number is not 2.

**One Step Further**
Think of a number. Give clues to a friend to help him or her guess the correct number.

Kindergarten Essentials

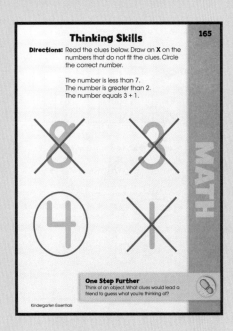

### 165 Thinking Skills

**Directions:** Read the clues below. Draw an **X** on the numbers that do not fit the clues. Circle the correct number.

The number is less than 7.
The number is greater than 2.
The number equals 3 + 1.

**One Step Further**
Think of an object. What clues would lead a friend to guess what you're thinking of?

Kindergarten Essentials

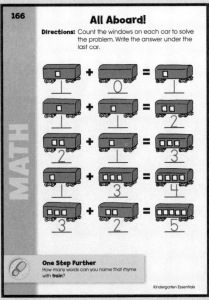

### 166 All Aboard!

**Directions:** Count the windows on each car to solve the problem. Write the answer under the last car.

**One Step Further**
How many words can you name that rhyme with **train**?

Kindergarten Essentials

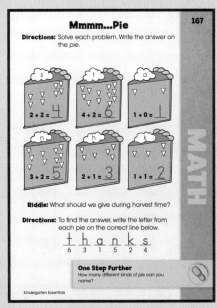

### 167 Mmmm...Pie

**Directions:** Solve each problem. Write the answer on the pie.

$2 + 2 = 4$  $4 + 2 = 6$  $1 + 0 = 1$
$3 + 2 = 5$  $2 + 1 = 3$  $1 + 1 = 2$

**Riddle:** What should we give during harvest time?

**Directions:** To find the answer, write the letter from each pie on the correct line below.

t h a n k s
6 3 1 5 2 4

**One Step Further**
How many different kinds of pie can you name?

Kindergarten Essentials

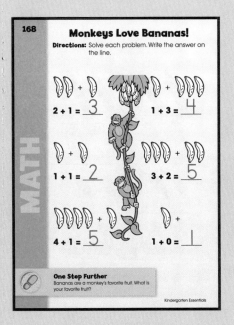

### 168 Monkeys Love Bananas!

**Directions:** Solve each problem. Write the answer on the line.

$2 + 1 = 3$  $1 + 3 = 4$
$1 + 1 = 2$  $3 + 2 = 5$
$4 + 1 = 5$  $1 + 0 = 1$

**One Step Further**
Bananas are a monkey's favorite fruit. What is your favorite fruit?

Kindergarten Essentials

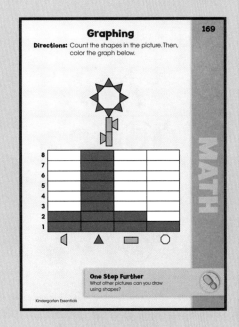

### 169 Graphing

**Directions:** Count the shapes in the picture. Then, color the graph below.

**One Step Further**
What other pictures can you draw using shapes?

Kindergarten Essentials

MATH

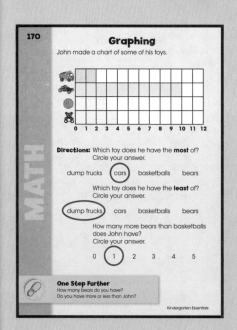

170

**Graphing**

John made a chart of some of his toys.

**Directions:** Which toy does he have the **most** of?
Circle your answer.

dump trucks (cars) basketballs bears

Which toy does he have the **least** of?
Circle your answer.

(dump trucks) cars basketballs bears

How many more bears than basketballs
does John have?
Circle your answer.

0 (1) 2 3 4 5

**One Step Further**
How many bears do you have?
Do you have more or less than John?

Kindergarten Essentials

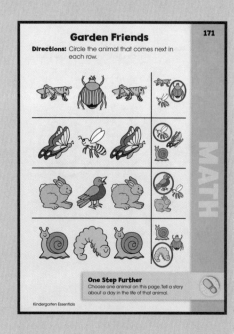

171

**Garden Friends**

**Directions:** Circle the animal that comes next in
each row.

**One Step Further**
Choose one animal on this page. Tell a story
about a day in the life of that animal.

Kindergarten Essentials

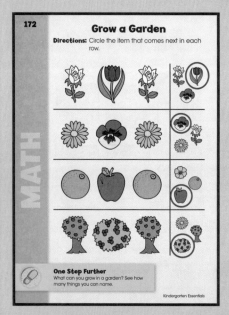

172

**Grow a Garden**

**Directions:** Circle the item that comes next in each
row.

**One Step Further**
What can you grow in a garden? See how
many things you can name.

Kindergarten Essentials

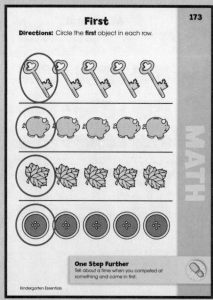

173

**First**

**Directions:** Circle the **first** object in each row.

**One Step Further**
Tell about a time when you competed at
something and came in first.

Kindergarten Essentials

174

**Second**

**Directions:** Circle the **second** object in each row.

**One Step Further**
Stand in line with three of your friends. Who is
second?

Kindergarten Essentials

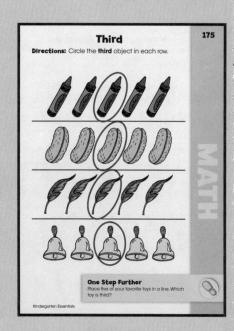

175

**Third**

**Directions:** Circle the **third** object in each row.

**One Step Further**
Place five of your favorite toys in a line. Which
toy is third?

Kindergarten Essentials

ANSWER KEY

**176** **Fourth**

**Directions:** Circle the **fourth** thing in each row.

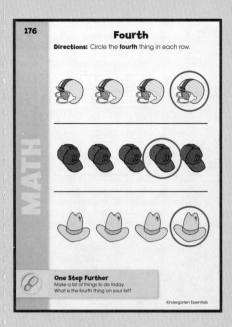

**One Step Further**
Make a list of things to do today.
What is the fourth thing on your list?

Kindergarten Essentials

**At the Fire Station** **177**

**Directions:** Color the squares. Then, color the rest of the picture.

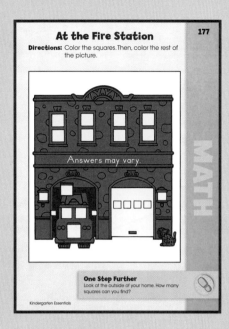

Answers may vary.

**One Step Further**
Look at the outside of your home. How many squares can you find?

Kindergarten Essentials

**178** **At the Train Yard**

**Directions:** Color the rectangles. Then, color the rest of the picture.

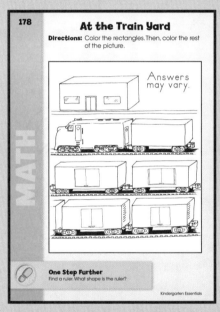

Answers may vary.

**One Step Further**
Find a ruler. What shape is the ruler?

Kindergarten Essentials

**Exploring the Garden** **179**

**Directions:** Color the circles and triangles. Then, color the rest of the picture.

Answers may vary.

**One Step Further**
Draw a triangle and a circle. Then, turn the shapes into drawings of animals.

Kindergarten Essentials

**180** **Fun on the Farm**

**Directions:** Find the circles, triangles, and squares and color them. Then, color the rest of the picture.

Answers may vary.

**One Step Further**
Imagine you have your very own farm. What would you grow on your farm?

Kindergarten Essentials

**182** **Colors**

**Directions:** Circle the words in the puzzle. The words go across and down.

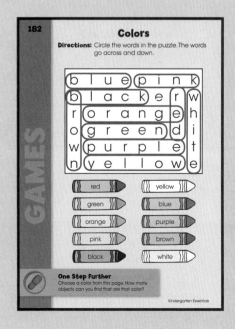

| red | yellow |
| green | blue |
| orange | purple |
| pink | brown |
| black | white |

**One Step Further**
Choose a color from this page. How many objects can you find that are that color?

Kindergarten Essentials

Kindergarten Essentials

ANSWER KEY

**Time for Art** 183

**Directions:** Help Anna find her drawing pad.

**One Step Further**
Draw a picture using at least five different colored crayons.

Kindergarten Essentials

**What Is Round?** 184

**Directions:** Circle the words in the puzzle. The words go across and down.

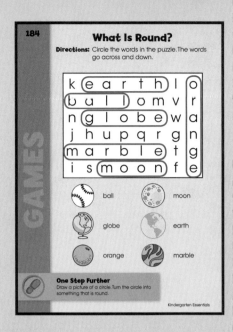

**One Step Further**
Draw a picture of a circle. Turn the circle into something that is round.

Kindergarten Essentials

**Swamp Search** 185

**Directions:** Color the circles to get to the swamp.

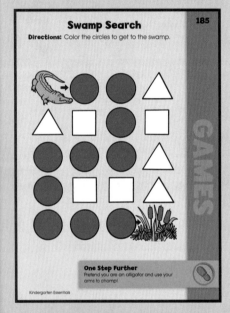

**One Step Further**
Pretend you are an alligator and use your arms to chomp!

Kindergarten Essentials

**Fun on Skis** 186

**Directions:** Help the skier down the mountain.

**One Step Further**
Which activity would you choose: swimming in the summer or skiing in the winter?

Kindergarten Essentials

**How Is the Weather?** 187

**Directions:** Circle the words in the puzzle. The words go across and down.

**One Step Further**
What is the weather like today? What is your favorite kind of weather?

Kindergarten Essentials

**The Lost Nest** 188

**Directions:** Help the dinosaur mother find her nest of eggs.

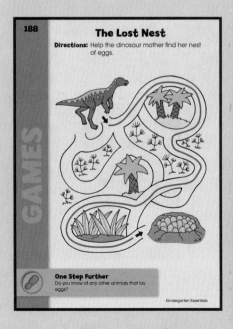

**One Step Further**
Do you know of any other animals that lay eggs?

Kindergarten Essentials

Kindergarten Essentials

### Dino Pet! 189
**Directions:** If you could have a pet dinosaur, what would it look like? Draw your dinosaur below.

Answers will vary.

**One Step Further**
Would you like to have a pet dinosaur? Why or why not?

Kindergarten Essentials

### 190 On the Farm
**Directions:** Circle the words in the puzzle. The words go across and down.

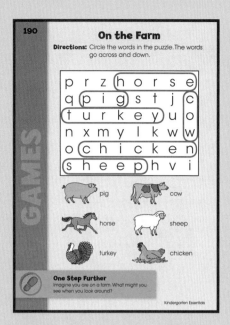

**One Step Further**
Imagine you are on a farm. What might you see when you look around?

Kindergarten Essentials

### Farm Babies 191
**Directions:** Help the babies find their mothers.

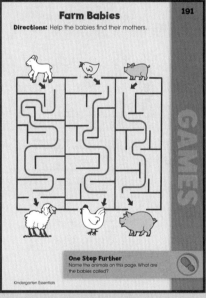

**One Step Further**
Name the animals on this page. What are the babies called?

Kindergarten Essentials

### 192 A Bone for Skipper
**Directions:** Help Skipper find the bone.

**One Step Further**
Design a doghouse for Skipper.

Kindergarten Essentials

### Pets 193
**Directions:** Circle the words in the puzzle. The words go across and down.

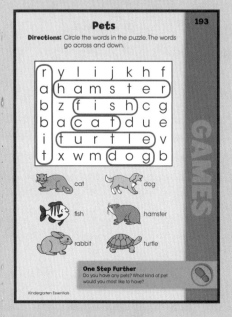

**One Step Further**
Do you have any pets? What kind of pet would you most like to have?

Kindergarten Essentials

### 194 A Leafy Path
**Directions:** Help the squirrel find its tree.

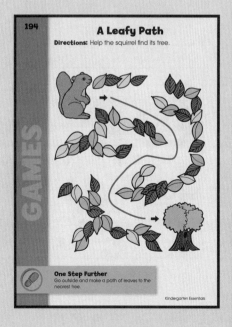

**One Step Further**
Go outside and make a path of leaves to the nearest tree.

Kindergarten Essentials

Kindergarten Essentials

ANSWER KEY

### Forest Babies    195
**Directions:** Help the babies find their mothers.

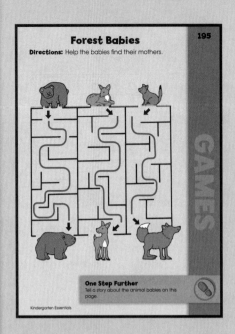

**One Step Further**
Tell a story about the animal babies on this page.

Kindergarten Essentials

### A New Home    196
**Directions:** Help the hermit crab find a new home.

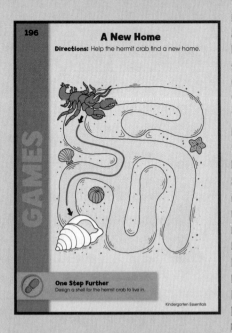

**One Step Further**
Design a shell for the hermit crab to live in.

Kindergarten Essentials

### In the Ocean    197
**Directions:** Circle the words in the puzzle. The words go across and down.

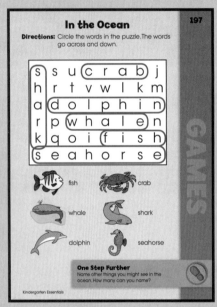

**One Step Further**
Name other things you might see in the ocean. How many can you name?

Kindergarten Essentials

### Learning the Past    198
**Directions:** Help the museum guide find the dinosaur display.

**One Step Further**
Do you like going to the museum? What is the most interesting thing you've seen?

Kindergarten Essentials

### Digging Up Bones    199
**Directions:** Help the scientist find the dinosaur bones.

**One Step Further**
Why do you think dinosaur bones are important?

Kindergarten Essentials

### School Tools    200
**Directions:** Circle the words in the puzzle. The words go across and down.

**One Step Further**
Look at the objects on this page. What else do you need for school?

Kindergarten Essentials

*Kindergarten Essentials*

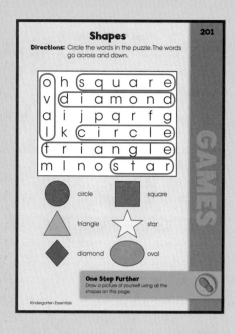

### Shapes
**201**

**Directions:** Circle the words in the puzzle. The words go across and down.

| o | h | s | q | u | a | r | e |
|---|---|---|---|---|---|---|---|
| v | d | i | a | m | o | n | d |
| a | i | j | p | q | r | f | g |
| l | k | c | i | r | c | l | e |
| t | r | i | a | n | g | l | e |
| m | l | n | o | s | t | a | r |

- circle
- square
- triangle
- star
- diamond
- oval

**One Step Further**
Draw a picture of yourself using all the shapes on this page.

Kindergarten Essentials

GAMES

---

### A Speedy Race
**202**

**Directions:** Help the race car get to the finish line.

FINISH

**One Step Further**
Pretend you are driving a race car. How fast do you go?

Kindergarten Essentials

GAMES

---

### In the Country
**203**

**Directions:** Circle the words in the puzzle. The words go across and down.

| d | b | z | w | u | v | y | h |
|---|---|---|---|---|---|---|---|
| a | r | f | i | e | l | d | i |
| c | i | x | t | o | w | n | l |
| b | d | p | m | q | e | r | l |
| b | g | r | o | a | d | s | t |
| o | e | m | e | a | d | o | w |

- hill
- road
- town
- field
- bridge
- meadow

**One Step Further**
Create your own word search using words of things you might see in the country.

Kindergarten Essentials

GAMES

---

### Living Things
**204**

**Directions:** Circle the words in the puzzle. The words go across and down.

| m | x | c | b | a | b | y | s |
|---|---|---|---|---|---|---|---|
| g | m | a | n | p | b | r | a |
| r | n | o | y | z | q | h | t |
| a | f | l | o | w | e | r | u |
| s | w | d | o | g | v | i | d |
| s | l | k | t | r | e | e | j |

- dog
- man
- tree
- baby
- grass
- flower

**One Step Further**
Name three more things that would fit in the "Living Things" category on this page.

Kindergarten Essentials

GAMES

---

### Nonliving Things
**205**

**Directions:** Circle the words in the puzzle. The words go across and down.

| g | y | c | l | b | s | k | c |
|---|---|---|---|---|---|---|---|
| c | b | o | o | k | h | m | l |
| a | b | a | l | l | j | t | o |
| r | z | f | a | i | u | n | c |
| d | p | e | n | c | i | l | k |
| e | x | d | o | l | l | v | w |

- car
- doll
- ball
- book
- clock
- pencil

**One Step Further**
Tell a story that includes at least three of the objects on this page.

Kindergarten Essentials

GAMES

---

### Time to Go!
**206**

**Directions:** Help the family get home.

**One Step Further**
Draw a map of the street you live on. See if a friend can find your home.

Kindergarten Essentials

GAMES

---

ANSWER KEY

### In the City 207

**Directions:** Circle the words in the puzzle. The words go across and down.

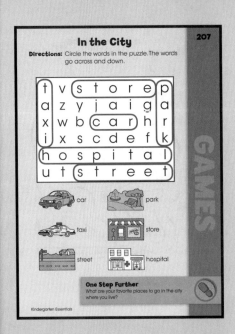

**One Step Further**
What are your favorite places to go in the city where you live?

Kindergarten Essentials

### 208 Find the Mistakes

**Directions:** Circle 5 mistakes that are in the picture.

**One Step Further**
Imagine you wake up one morning and everything is backward! Tell a story about it.

Kindergarten Essentials

### On Land 209

**Directions:** Circle the words in the puzzle. The words go across and down.

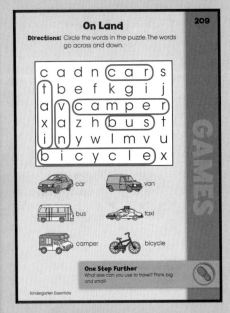

**One Step Further**
What else can you use to travel? Think big and small!

Kindergarten Essentials

### 210 A Garden Helper

**Directions:** Help the girl find her flower garden.

**One Step Further**
How many different types of flowers can you name?

Kindergarten Essentials

### Bugs 211

**Directions:** Circle the words in the puzzle. The words go across and down.

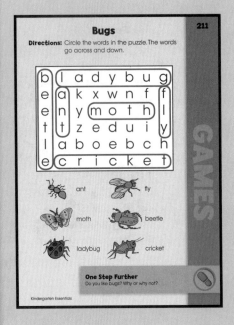

**One Step Further**
Do you like bugs? Why or why not?

Kindergarten Essentials

### 212 At the Zoo

**Directions:** Circle the words in the puzzle. The words go across and down.

**One Step Further**
Draw a picture of a day at the zoo. Tell a story about your picture.

Kindergarten Essentials

## Let's Go to the Zoo 213

**Directions:** Help the family find their way to the zoo.

**One Step Further**
Tell a story about a day at the zoo. What animals did you see?

Kindergarten Essentials

## 214 Community Helpers

**Directions:** Circle the words in the puzzle. The words go across and down.

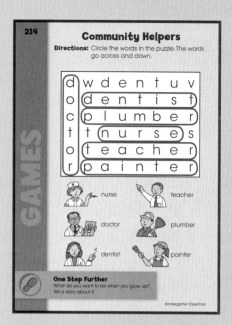

**One Step Further**
What do you want to be when you grow up? Tell a story about it.

Kindergarten Essentials

## Money 215

**Directions:** Circle the words in the puzzle. The words go across and down.

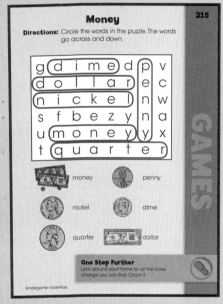

**One Step Further**
Look around your home for all the loose change you can find. Count it.

Kindergarten Essentials

## 216 Polar Bear Palace

**Directions:** Circle **6** mistakes that are in the picture.

**One Step Further**
If you were a polar bear, what would you do all day?

Kindergarten Essentials

## A Lost Mitten 217

**Directions:** Help the girl find her mitten.

**One Step Further**
Design a cool pair of mittens to wear in the winter.

Kindergarten Essentials

## 218 In the Air

**Directions:** Circle the words in the puzzle. The words go across and down.

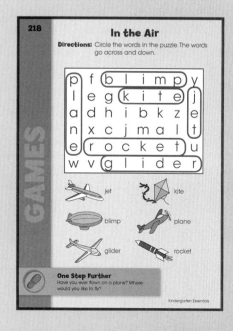

**One Step Further**
Have you ever flown on a plane? Where would you like to fly?

Kindergarten Essentials

**ANSWER KEY**

Kindergarten Essentials

256